On the Water

MEMBER FISHING TIPS

North American Fishing Club
Minnetonka, MN

≋ ACKNOWLEDGEMENTS ≋

On the Water—Member Fishing Tips

Printed in 2005.

It takes many people to create a book like this, but some deserve a **special thank-you**. First—thanks to all the NAFC members who took time to send tips, ideas, pictures and illustrations; this book started with you! Next—thanks to Glenn Sapir, long-time outdoor writer and friend of the NAFC, who waded through the hundreds upon hundreds of member contributions that came in. And finally, a thank you to Teresa Marrone who pulled everything together into the pages that follow.

Tom Carpenter
Creative Director

Michele Stockham
Senior Book Development Coordinator

Teresa Marrone, BatScanner Productions
Book Production & Design

Glenn Sapir
Tip Editor

Bill Lindner Photography
Dan Kennedy
Photographers

Dave Rottinghaus
Joe Tomelleri
Illustrators

7 8 9 10 11 12 / 10 09 08 07 06 05
© 2001 North American Fishing Club
ISBN 1-58159-083-0

North American Fishing Club
12301 Whitewater Drive
Minnetonka, MN 55343
www.fishingclub.com

Table of Contents

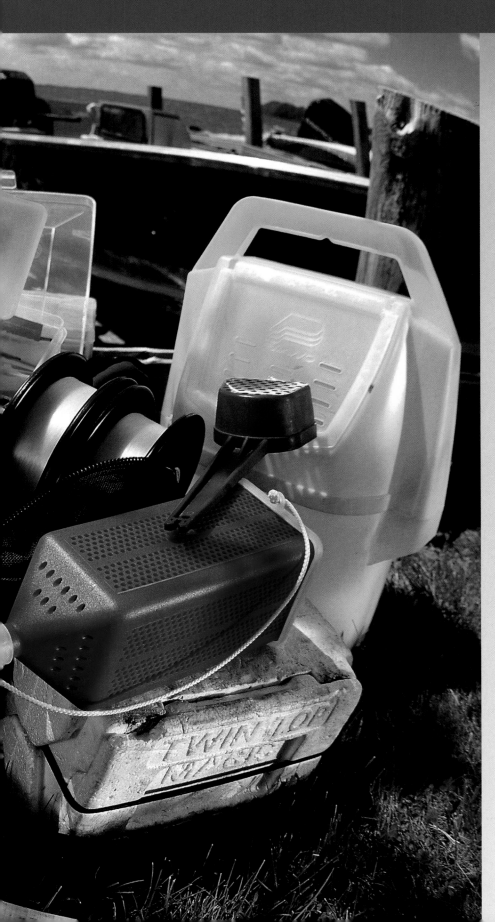

Whether you've been fishing for one year or a hundred, you've discovered by now that ours is a game of details ...

Fishing the right place at the right time. Using your rods and reels to their full and maximum efficiency. Keeping all your tackle and gear in excellent working order. Tying knots that will hold under tough conditions. Making sure you're using the right terminal tackle for the task at hand. Selecting baits that will attract the fish you're after. Taking care of the myriad "little things" that make or break your fishing success.

And we all know there's one place where these lessons are best learned: on the water. That's where you can investigate, manipulate, cogitate ... try the different things that might bring you more fishing success. But who wants to spend all their fishing time experimenting? Fishing time is time to catch fish!

One way to take a little and acceptable shortcut to more fishing success is to tap on the experience of others—real fishermen who, like you, fish really hard and are willing to share their ideas.

That's what we've brought together for you in *On the Water—Member Fishing Tips*. On these pages are hundreds of years' worth of fishing wisdom, clearly and concisely explained and illustrated for your fishing benefit. Members were kind enough to share much of the knowledge here, but we also got contributions from experts associated with the North American Fishing Club, and even prepared a special bonus section on customizing your own fishing boat.

You could spend a lot of time on the water, figuring out the great ideas in this book for yourself. But why not take it easy on yourself? No matter how long you've been fishing or where you fish or what you fish for, there are ideas here that will save you time, make your fishing more fun and, simply enough, help you catch more fish.

And who can argue with a bottom line like that?

See ya on the water.

There's a lot more to rod-and-reel care then, well, no care at all. Because that's what many of us do—just place these expensive, precision pieces of equipment in a corner and expect them to perform flawlessly next time out on the water. It doesn't work that way—so here are members' tips and ideas for taking care of this important business: the maintenance of some of your most important fishing tools.

The topic isn't romantic, to be sure, but neither is an equipment failure you could have easily and economically prevented.

RODS & REELS

Rod Holder/ Gear Carrier

When bank fishing, I have often found myself at a loss for a spot to put a rod holder in the ground (especially at a pier). To remedy this, I use a plastic milk crate I bought very cheaply at a flea market. With the milk crate between me and the water, I attach two clamp-on-type rod holders to the crate rim nearest to me. With the rods in the holders reaching across the crate, a fish on the line will not upset the crate as it would if the rod holders were mounted across on the opposite lip. The crate also makes a handy tote for loose gear.

William Evans
Frankton, IN

Superline for Rod Repair

Don't throw away those last few yards of superline once you've filled your spool. Keep that braided line in your tackle box, along with a tube of industrial glue. I happened to have broken one of my favorite rods while up in Canada a few years ago, fishing for pike and walleye. My spinning rod broke at the rod seat. Whether it was because I tightened it down too much or because of the repeated stress of good strikes or a combination of both, I don't know. The portion of the rod that screws down on the reel broke, leaving my reel loose on the rod. Any pressure made the crack worse.

To repair the rod, I put a bead of glue around the end of the broken reel seat and in the offending crack, then wrapped some spare superline around it, keeping it tight so the crack closed up. Once the glue started getting stiff, I put in another bead of glue and kept wrapping until there was about $\frac{1}{16}$ inch of line around the broken reel seat. Another bead of glue made sure the glue would soak in all around, and I left it overnight to cure.

That was 5 years ago, and it's still my favorite rod.

Frank Russo
Pompton Lakes, NJ

Basic Reel Maintenance

Having been in the reel-repair business for many years, I know what people might do to abuse their tackle. I fished salt and fresh water for a long time, and I still use some of those first reels in salt water. We learned to take care of them, and that meant cleaning and oiling them immediately after each trip—not the next day!

James A. Sorrell
Edgewood, KY

It's in the Bag

An inexpensive dust cover for your reels is the plastic bag in which your newspaper is delivered when it rains or snows. Just slip the rod butt and reel in, then secure it with a rubberband or twist-tie, and you're all set.

James M. Brandenburg
Taos, NM

Easy Rod Hook Holder

If your rod does not have a line hook, you can go to your local electrical supply store and purchase plastic cable ties that have an eye on them. All you have to do is place one on the rod and snug it up. I have used them on a number of rods. They work great and are inexpensive.

Tex W. Davis
Centreville, VA

RODS & REELS

Olive Oil for Your Rod?

When your fishing rod is not in use, spray a paper towel with olive oil and rub down your entire rod, including the cork handle. This retards cracking and allows the rod to perform smoothly.

Leman Wilson
Vacaville, CA

Recycle Broken Rods

Save those broken rod tips. Glue or epoxy a 2- to 3-foot section of a broken rod tip into a ¼-inch drilled hole in a 1-inch-diameter wooden dowel. Clamp on a reel, and you have a custom ice fishing rod.

Matt Radzialowski
Wixom, MI

Wax for Distance

A way to get more distance on your casting is to apply car wax to the insides of your line guides. After you buff them, they will be as slick as ice and your line will slide through the glides.

Aaron Turner
Presque Isle, MI

Slowing Down Superlines

When using superlines, the arbor often turns without retrieving the line. You might think that your drag mechanism isn't working properly, but that's not the case.

To solve this problem, I put a rubber band around the arbor, then put the superline over the rubber band. This way you won't need monofilament for backing.

Merle Richardson
Rhinelander, WI

Clean Old Tackle

Here's a good way to clean corrosion from old reels and rods that have been used in salt water. Put some white vinegar in a bowl and soak a toothbrush in it (use a hard-bristle brush). Dip the brush in the vinegar and scrub the corrosion on the rod or reel. Rinse off with clean water. I like to wipe them with WD-40. I buy a lot of old rods and reels at public auctions, and after they are cleaned up, I have nice outfits for next to nothing.

John Wealand
Conestoga, PA

Sock It to Your Reels

Here's an easy-to-make reel cover. Take an old tube sock, cut off the toes and slide your reel into it. You can secure the reel with a twist-tie or a rubber band at each end.

Tim Rehwald
Lawrenceville, IL

≈ ADVICE FROM THE PROS ≈

Backlash Help

No fishing time is more wasted than that spent picking out backlashes. Here are two tips to reduce this bane.

First, the second you get a backlash, place your thumb firmly on the spool line and make several complete handle turns. Ninety percent of those "muss-ups" will easily unravel.

Second, braided lines make impossible-to-pick-out backlashes because the slick line cuts through to the spool axle. To thwart this, make your longest cast, then place a strip of plastic tape across the line. Retrieve, winding over the tape, and that's as deep as any backlash can penetrate, making "pickouts" easier.

Gene Round
Ocala, FL

Library for Your Fishing Reels

When I buy a new reel, the factory sends a parts diagram with an exploded view. Unfortunately, the diagrams are usually so small I can't recognize the parts. With an enlarging copy machine, I blow up the diagrams to a standard page size. Put the diagrams and factory specifications in a three-ring binder with plastic page protectors. All your reel specifications (with legible diagrams), warrantees, receipts and factory recommendations are well organized and ready to help you maintain your equipment.

William L. McCabe
Napa, CA

Wash Your Rods and Reels

Here's something to do when you are not on the water.

Wash your rods and reels in warm soapy water. Dry them, then give them a coat of automotive wax to protect them. Use toothpaste and toothbrushes on cork foam-rubber handles to remove built-up dirt.

William J. Beacham
Dundas, Ontario, Canada

Clean Your Reel

Cleaning and oiling a fishing reel can be simplified. First, take the reel apart and lay out the pieces on a sheet of waxed paper. Next, wipe the pieces off with a clean, lint-free cloth. Then use a spray cleaner designed for cleaning electronic components (it doesn't have any chemicals that will harm the surface) such as Endust for Electronics. Wipe the pieces thoroughly with a clean, lint-free cloth. Then use a white lithium-based grease for the gears and other areas that need greasing. Last, put the reel back together and spray it with a silicone-based lubricant. The lubricant penetrates throughout the reel and lasts for a long time.

Xavier V. McClung
Valdosta, GA

Protect Rods in a Boat

Having rods get nicked when coming in and out of a boat's storage compartment really bugs me, so here is what I do to prevent the problem:

First, clean the rods, then polish them with a paste wax, such as Johnson's. The paste wax protects all rod materials, including the cork. To clean the cork handles, lightly apply a fine sandpaper. Then polish the cork, too, with the paste wax for a brand-new, nonslippery appearance.

Next, buy rolled felt (at a fabric or department store) that is 3 inches or so in width. For spinning rods with particularly large guides, you may need even wider felt. Sew the top and sides, and you have socks for your rods. They protect your rods when in use and come off easily when you are ready to put the rods to work.

Joseph J. Karpus
Burbank, IL

Keep a Cleaning Cloth Handy

I keep an old piece of cotton sheet in my tackle box. It has been heavily sprayed with silicone spray. I use it to polish spoons and to wipe down my rods and reels at the end of each outing, after rinsing them down with fresh water. This keeps the reel from rusting and makes for longer casts with clean rod guides.

Ross Gough
Key West, FL

Lubricate Your Reel—and Line

When they are not in use, spray your fishing reel, including the line, with WD-40 and put it away. The next time you use it you'll notice how smooth the outfit works. The WD-40 also keeps your line from getting brittle.

Leman Wilson
Vacaville, CA

With all the fancy-schmancy jigs, crankbaits, spoons, soft-plastics, spinners and what-not available today, it's a wonder live and natural bait ever finds its way onto a fish hook.

But most of us use natural bait at one time or another, just because it works, and some of us wouldn't dream of going anywhere near a lake, reservoir, pond, river or creek without something live and wiggly (or maybe even smelly) to impale on a hook.

Here's how to get the most out of your natural baits ... and catch more fish with them.

NATURAL BAIT

Who Needs Stink Baits

I use aftershave or cologne to scent my dough balls for carp. It is quick and easy—it works great too!

Joe Tury
Warren, OH

Double-Set Your Hook

When bait fishing for tough-mouthed fish (catfish, sturgeon, stripers, shark, etc.), it pays to "double-set" your hook. When you first notice your rod tip acting suspicious, pick up your rod and point the tip directly toward the fish. At the next nudge from the fish, give your reel a quick turn. When you feel weight, snap the rod to the 12 o'clock position. Quickly drop your rod to the water with a turn of your reel, set the hook again and hold on. You will land more fish with the double hookset.

William L. McCabe
Napa, CA

Short-Strike Remedy

When short-striking walleyes keep nipping the tail of your minnow and stealing your bait, a trailer hook is a logical solution. From my experience, most of the time that I add a trailer hook I lose the strikes. To combat this, I put on a very small minnow or half of a nightcrawler, and I sometimes even replace the jig with a hook and split-shot.

Jeff Grzeskowiak
Marysville, OH

Make Worms Float

To make my nightcrawlers float, I break them in half and thread the crawler halfway up the worm on a No. 6 hook. Then, after buying a syringe with the smallest needle available at pet or feed stores, I inject air in the worm to make it float off the bottom.

Lyle J. Kelsey
Fallbrook, CA

Free Bait

Next time you are on a lake that is experiencing a massive shad kill—which usually occurs when shad are in shallow, cold water—scoop them up with your landing net and later cut them into bait-size pieces and freeze them. It's excellent catfish bait or chum, and it beats paying $3 or more at the store. Be sure, however, of the relevant bait-harvesting laws before collecting the shad.

Jeff Grzeskowiak
Marysville, OH

Bait Needle Holder

I enjoy fishing for trout using minnows, which I "thread" on the line using a minnow needle. To carry spare needles in my fishing vest I use an old cartridge ink pen. Just remove the cap, and a needle is readily available. The pen can be carried loose in any pocket or clipped onto a shirt pocket.

Donald Dickison
Portland, PA

Match Bait Size for Salmon

When large schools of baitfish begin to show up while salmon fishing, pay attention to the size of the bait. Packaged anchovies and herring are usually mature fish. They can be twice the size of the bait-fish on which the salmon are feeding. Cut your pack-aged bait down to match the size of the bait in the water. It will result in more strikes.

For trolling, cut the head off at an angle (called a cut plug), leaving the body and tail about the size of the natural bait. For mooching, cut out a sec-tion between the head and the tail to bring it to the correct size.

You will pick up more fish using the right-size bait.

William L. McCabe
Napa, CA

Chicken Delight

To quickly trap a full load of minnows, place a fried chicken leg in your minnow trap. It works great.

Also, I dip my bait in fried chicken oil. It has improved my catch.

James R. Bryant
Attalla, AL

Add Milk to Your Herring

Salmon fishermen know that salting herring overnight before fishing is a good way to toughen the bait so that they will stay on the hook well. The salt may also add a smell to attract salmon. Unfortunately, herring will often dry out and shrivel when salt is added.

To prevent this, and to give your herring an attractive sheen, add a small can of evaporated milk when you salt them. The salt will still toughen the herring, but the milk will prevent them from shriveling up.

William Brown
Juneau, AK

Your Own Worm Supply

You can have live nightcrawlers and worms anytime you want them in spring or summer, and you don't have to pay the high cost of bait. Furthermore, at times when bait shops don't have crawlers or worms because of lengthy droughts, for example, you will have an ample supply. You simply need to raise them yourself.

To do this, dig a hole in the ground that extends below the frost level. Install a 60-gallon trash can in the hole. Mix moist leaves, used coffee grounds and worm food, then place the mixture in the trash can. Finally, put your initial investment of worms and/or nightcrawlers in the trash can.

A few things to remember: Never use oak leaves or grass clippings; remove dead nightcrawlers or worms; and keep leaves moist, but not wet.

Gary Hagadone
Waterford, MI

Worm Saver

Have trouble keeping worms alive on long trips? Boy, I did-—until I saw my grandma working in the garden. She used potting mix and she complained that she couldn't keep the worms out of it. Bingo! I had an idea. Put my worms in the potting mix! It's easy and cheap. Get yourself a bag of potting soil. A 10-pound bag lasts a long time. Also, get a bag of vermiculite. Mix about 2 cups of vermiculite into about 5 pounds of potting soil and put it in a clean 5-gallon paint bucket or other lidded bucket. Put in your worms and add another 2 or 3 inches of the potting soil. Keep moist, and your worms will stay fresh.

Sean Wilson
San Bernardino, CA

Liver Stable

Chicken livers are a great bait for catfish, but they often fall off the hook. To counter this problem, put the chicken livers in strawberry-banana Jell-O and let them sit for at least 24 hours. Afterward, the livers will stay on the hook better.

Jimmy Sampson
Huntsville, AL

Crayfish Tie

Improve your crayfish baiting by twisting one or two garbage-bag wire ties around the hook and then around the crayfish. Bare the wire for a stealthier set-up.

Dennis Malkin
Gates Mills, OH

Sweeten Your Pork

Adding a little anise oil and a spoonful of garlic powder to your jars of pork rind will help lure in the bass. The longer the rind soaks in the mixture, the better it will perform.

Leslie J. Richardson
San Benito, TX

Baitfish Hardiness Chart

Extremely Hardy	Moderately Hardy	Somewhat Hardy	Least Hardy
American eel	Blacknose dace	Banded killifish	Alewife
Mudminnow	Bluegill	Common shiner	Cisco
Fathead minnow	Bluntnose minnow	Red shiner	Emerald shiner
Mudtom	Creek chub	Yellow perch	Gizzard shad
	Fine-scale dace		Rainbow smelt
	Goldfish		Spottail shiner
	Horyhead chub		
	Mottled sculpin		
	Southern redbelly dace		
	White sucker		

Stan Ludorf
Granby, CT

Bait-Fishing Strike Indicator

While bait fishing, I know my eyes often wander. That caused me to miss hits. One day, while messing around with my tackle, I discovered how to see a hit without watching the tip of the rod.

I took a long bobber and hooked it on my line between the bottom guide—that is, the largest—and the next guide. Then I would let the float hang as I waited.

Using this method, when you get a bite, the bobber will rise as the slack becomes scarce.

Then I set the hook, unclip the bobber and try to reel in the fish.

I hope this tip may help bait fishermen catch some fish, despite their wandering eyes.

Bryan Schellenger
Chugiak, AK

Stink Bait from Family Freezer

I don't like to buy bait for catfish. Instead, I look in the freezer and find some old meat that has gotten pushed to the bottom. I let the meat thaw, then I cut it into pieces for use. I even put some back into the freezer for future use. The longer I leave the meat out, the more it smells like stink bait.

Scott Torbeck
St. Peter, IL

A Bait Needle for Catfishermen

If you catfish with chicken livers, you know what a problem that can be. You make your cast and half the bait goes flying through the air. Well, here's a solution to the problem.

Take a 6-inch piece of straight, thin wire—a paper clip will work—and about 1 inch from an end, make a loop by bending the wire. Snug the tag end to the main wire. Tie a leader onto a size 10 or larger treble hook. Slip the leader loop onto the loop in the wire. Now you have a "needle and thread." Darn the needle through a chunk of liver and slide the liver down onto the hook. Most of the liver will be threaded onto the leader and clinched at the end by the treble hook. This should end bait coming loose on the cast.

Steve Arbayo
Pioneertown, CA

Coffee Can Leech Trap

Here's how to create a neat device for catching leeches for bait:

Add a few fresh fish heads and some small rocks to the bottom of an empty 2-pound coffee can. Squeeze together the top of the can to form a narrow opening. Drill a couple of small holes near the top of the can, tie one end of a small rope to the can through the holes, then attach an empty jug to the other end of the rope as a marker buoy. Toss the can into a weedbed or tie off to a dock.

Check the trap once a day for leeches and replace the fish heads with fresh ones every couple of days.

Matt Radzialowski
Wixom, MI

Minnow Rig Fishing for Perch

When fishing for yellow perch with a minnow rig, you may, at times, get stuck using a soft-tipped rod that makes it hard to both feel strikes and make a hookup. In this situation, it may be best just to let your minnow rest, slack lined, on the bottom for a minute or more.

If there is a school of perch nearby, you have about a 50-50 chance that a perch will swallow your minnow. This method, of course, should only be used when you intend to keep your fish.

Alan Vormelker
Cleveland, OH

How to Rig Flying Fish

Use 300-pound-test wire as your harness to rig flying fish. Rig the harness through the eyes, then into the "wings". Use an 8/0 to 9/0 hook rig. The lead hook is above the wing; the trailing hook is in the tail. Stitch the fish to keep the lead hook in the bait. This is a particularly effective West Coast rig for big tuna and for marlin.

Harold L. Houser
Santa Barbara, CA

Minnow Saver

To keep minnows alive for several weeks at a time, put the minnows in your minnow bucket with just enough water to cover them, then store the minnow bucket in your refrigerator. The minnows will face in the same direction as they swim, creating a current in the water that keeps the water oxygenated. Do not try to feed the minnows; the food will foul the water. When you take them on your fishing trip, keep them cool. Place the minnow bucket in a cooler on top of ice or add ice to the bucket periodically during the day.

Steven Hunt
Baltimore, MD

Do Blonds Catch More Fish?

If you are a live-bait fisherman, dump a couple of capfuls of hydrogen peroxide into the bait live well. Your bait will stay alive longer, especially on hot days. (Don't get any on your hair, unless, of course, you are already blond.)

William Picking
Monson, MA

NATURAL BAIT

Beware of Flying Liver

A "bait bag" is another neat way to keep chicken livers on your hook when fishing for cats. There are two ways you can make it:

First, take a tiny, 1- to 2-inch square, zippered plastic bag and punch little pencil holes in it. Stuff it with a chunk of liver. Now, just hook the bag anywhere and cast. No more lost bait, and when the cat takes the bag, he takes the hook too.

Another method of making a bait bag is to use nylon stocking or small-mesh material. Cut some 2- x 4-inch pieces, fold them in half and stitch them on two sides, leaving an opening. Weave a piece of thread around the opening so you have a drawstring. You now have some 2-inch-square bait bags that will ooze scent and keep your bait on the hook. Just stuff the bag, tie the drawstring, hook the bag and cast.

Steve Arbayo
Pioneertown, CA

Eyes Have It

Use industrial-strength glue to attach small eyes onto worms, grubs, leadhead jigs or even crankbaits. After reading a study that stated fish will often key in on their prey's eyes, I felt this addition would improve my chances of enticing a strike from finicky fish. It really works and is clearly a good idea. Many lure manufacturers are making soft baits with such eyes. I use small arts-and-crafts eyes purchased from Wal-Mart.

Richard K. Stratton
Massena, NY

Beans for Bullheads

If you take kids fishing, go for bullheads. It is one of the easiest fish for kids to catch. A bait that is not only effective, but is also easy for the kids to put on themselves, is canned lima beans. This bait is cheap and keeps forever … even in the hot sun.

Bruce Walters
Horseheads, NY

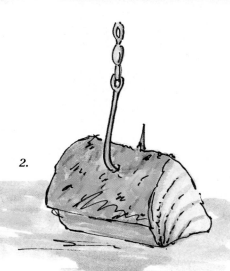

Baiting a Chunk

Here are simple step-by-step illustrations on rigging a chunk bait. This rig is effective on all coasts, but I find it to be particularly deadly on big tuna on the West Coast.

1. Cut a chunk of bait about 1 to 1½ inches wide and 2½ to 3½ inches long. Into that chunk cut a ¾-inch slit.
2. Insert hook into slit.
3. Turn the hook back toward the chunk. Reinsert the hook point and a small portion of the bend, so that the point is hidden, but not buried so deeply that hooking the fish would be difficult. If you are using a swiveling hook, be sure to keep the swivel outside the chunk so that the hook may continue to turn freely.

Harold L. Houser
Santa Barbara, CA

You Gotta Have Heart

I find that two tubs of chicken livers bought at a store (not fresh) and mixed with 1 pound of chicken hearts (marinated overnight), will make the chicken hearts taste and smell like chicken livers. The chicken hearts, however, are harder to get off the hook, and the catfish love them.

Joseph Wainscott
Harrison, OH

Check Corn Fields for Sucker Bait

In early spring when you want to go sucker fishing, it can sometimes be hard to get bait. All you need do is go to a corn stubble field, pull the stalks out of the ground and shake them. You will find enough "dew worms" to keep you fishing.

Only take as many as you'll need and leave the rest for other fishermen and for your next fishing trip.

Paul L. Winstead Jr.
Mt. Vernon, OH

Spawn Bag Help

Here in Michigan, spawn bags are a very popular springtime bait for steelhead and brown trout. Unfortunately, the cold water often fades and discolors the spawn. One way to help keep the spawn looking fresh is to sprinkle the eggs with Jello in its powder form before tying the roe into spawn bags. I recommend using natural color Jello mix—reds and oranges. Strawberry Jello mix on steelhead spawn works best for me.

Matt Radzialowski
Wixom, MI

Light Up Your Minnow Rig

At night, when the perch bite slows or stops, try to prolong your success by adding some type of fluorescent attractant to your minnow rig. Soft-plastic glow-in-the-dark bait substitutes work great, but remember to charge them with your flashlight.

Alan Vormelker
Cleveland, OH

Get More Minnows into Your Round Trap

To lure more minnows into my round trap, I add a few special touches that work really well.

I use the small cubes of aquarium fish food, designed to be pressed onto the inside glass of a fish tank. My favorite is the kind made from freeze-dried worms. With the trap apart, wet the cubes and pinch them between the tight wire mesh on the inside cones near the small openings. Bait both ends; I use two cubes per end. Once the minnows discover this enticement, it will create a traffic jam near the entrance, forcing much of the bait into the trap.

For added attraction, you can spray the cones with your favorite scent or attractant. Mine is worm or crawfish. Be sure to spray from the inside out, with the trap apart, to avoid getting spray on the sides of the trap. Remember, you want the minnows headed for the door, not the sides.

At night, put a small cyalume lightstick inside the trap. You can also attach the metal clip on top of the trap to the handle of a plastic jug so it will float just below the surface.

Jim Minnick
Niagara Falls, NY

Bait from Ragweed

In mid to late summer, you may find that a worm has bored a hole into a ragweed stalk and is living inside it. Panfish love these worms.

When you find stalks that have a hole in them, simply cut the stalks about 6 inches above and below the hole and take them with you. When you are ready to rig one, carefully split the stalk beginning at one end and use your finger to continue the split until you find the worm.

Paul L. Winstead Jr.
Mt. Vernon, OH

Shrimp for Cats

If you like catfishing, stop at the market and get yourself some fresh or frozen jumbo shrimp. Toss one out on a large hook and wait a while. Catfish love them. What you don't use can be enjoyed with some seafood sauce.

William Picking
Monson, MA

Keep Crawlers Crawling

For keeping worms and nightcrawlers tough and lively, I keep them in a foam-plastic cooler and use loose-weave white cotton dish cloths for bedding. I soak the dish cloths before using them to get rid of any filler, wring out excess water and put them all crumpled up in the cooler. This provides moisture, bedding and even food. No additional feeding is necessary. Worms and crawlers will become livelier and tougher in a couple of days.

I keep the cooler outside in the shade, inserting a reusable freezer pack on hot days. I also use a smaller foam-plastic cooler with dish cloths to use for my day trips.

Dish cloths should be taken out and rinsed every two or three weeks. Be sure they do not dry out!

Ross Gough
Key West, FL

Hose Your Catfish

To keep chicken or other meat liver baits on the hook, use panty hose! Wrap the liver in a small piece of discarded panty hose material. It lets the flavor seep into the water, driving the fish crazy. The liver lasts longer because it doesn't fall off during your cast.

Ben Lira
Lafayette, IN

Use Perch for Perch

Next time that big school of yellow perch uses up all of your bait, give this a try—if it is legal in your state or province. Fillet a small perch and skin it. Cut the fillet into quarters, and rig one of those quarters for bait.

Rex Ballard
Benzonia, MI

Dough Bait Recipe

Here's a great alternative to the chicken livers that fly off your hook on the cast or get pulled off by the smaller cats. It's a dough bait better than any of those premade mixes you can buy in the bait shop.

1. Grind 1 handful of dry cat food to powder.

2. Puree 1 chicken liver in the blender to a bloody liquid.

3. Add 1 egg to the blender and blend that in as well.

4. Combine the powdered cat food with the egg and liver.

5. Mold this concoction in your hands until a soft dough forms.

6. Add flour and knead the dough until it becomes very hard.

7. Keep above 32°F but below 45°F until use. Never freeze.

I got the idea when I tried a new body of water for carp using a dough bait with just flour, water and anise and caught only a few channel cats and no carp. Then I came back the next day and caught a large number on chicken liver; but the problem was, when I cast out, the liver would fly off the hook before it hit the water. So that night I came up with this bait, and the next day caught even more channel cats than the day before. This dough stays on the hook very well, even in strong river currents.

Pat
Via e-mail

Brings Worms to the Surface

When nightcrawlers and worms retreat deep into the earth during hot, dry weather, you can bring them to the surface by letting a hose run on the ground for about 20 minutes in the evening. Good fishing worms will emerge from the surface within minutes.

Jacob Sheehan
Eastford, CT

Corny Flounder Chum

If you fish for flounder from a boat, toss some kernels of yellow corn in the water. Let the corn and its scent travel down current for a while. If the current or tide is strong, and you are using heavy weights, paint them yellow. In any case, bait up with the yellow corn. Flounder, for some reason, are attracted to yellow.

William Picking
Monson, MA

Save Minnows and Crawlers with Weedless Hooks

A plain weedless hook, in place of a regular bait hook, can help prevent small fish from escaping with your minnows and nightcrawlers. Furthermore, I've found that minnows stay active longer if only hooked through the lip, and with this weedless hook method, you do not have to hook the worm or minnow numerous times.

Simply hook the minnow or worm, then snap the wire guard onto the turn of the hook by the barb. This keeps the bait on and helps prevent snagging or losing your bait in weedy or rocky areas. The larger gap created by the wire guard also keeps the smaller fish from getting their mouth on and chewing away at the bait. Hopefully, this allows the larger fish to get at it.

Matt Gregory
Palatine, IL

It's a wonder some fishermen can even jam themselves into their boat, what with the pounds of artificial lures (of every make, color and description imaginable) aboard.

But all artificial lures are not made alike ... nor are they fished alike. Each needs a different strategy and technique, and it's not always easy figuring out the nuances. These tips will give you an advantage on the water—showing you exactly how members and pros make sure they get the most fish-catching action out of their artificial baits.

When you're not catching fish, don't keep doing the same old thing. Alter your strategies and techniques with ideas like these.

Weighting Minnow Lures

Wrapping several coils of solder around the rear hook shank of a floating minnow lure will make the bait float tail down. Wrapping the center hook shank will cause a minnow lure to suspend. These variations can drive bass wild.

One caution: Do not use acid-filled solder because it can cause corrosion; use solid-wire solder with no flux.

Michael Baer
Hazard, KY

Double-Skirted Spinnerbaits

To make your spinnerbait work closer to the surface or sink more slowly, slip a skirt behind the original one. Besides adding more bulk and weight to the lure, the second skirt may attract larger fish.

Branden Maehr
Santa Margarita, CA

The Ultimate of Ultralight

Using ⅛₄-, ⅟₁₀₀- and ⅟₆₄-ounce jigheads, tie on your basic nymph and wet fly patterns. Best results are had by using 2-pound test or less, in order to get the jig where you want it. Most effective patterns have been Hare's Ear, Woollybugger and Beetles.

From dead drifting, bottom bouncing and slow twitch-and-retrieve, I've caught my limit dozens of times. Panfish and even bedded bass cannot resist a well-placed bug. Rainbows, browns and brookies are sure things.

Peter Arakawa
North Brunswick, NJ

Suction-Cup Poppers

If you want to add splash to any topwater bait, try this method I have devised: At a grocery or hardware store, buy various-size suction cups that are used on windows and mirrors for hanging items. Cut off the non-suction part of the item. Now, slit a hole through the center of the suction cup. Press the eyelet of any surface lure through the slit. Add a split ring to the portion of the eyelet that was pushed through the suction cup.

This modification has caught more bass for me than any of my high-priced poppers.

Andre L. Pineda
Irvine, CA

Sticky Jerkbait Idea

Industrial-strength glue on the hook eye will keep soft jerkbaits from sliding down the hook and make your baits last longer.

Jeffrey J. Knight
Fayetteville, NC

≋ ADVICE FROM THE PROS ≋

Tuning Baits for Docks

There are times of the day when bass hang out under docks. The pros can skip lures underneath with amazing skill. If you don't have that talent, try this: Take a big-lip crankbait and make it go under the dock. Say you're fishing the right side of the dock; use a pair of long-nose pliers to bend the lure's line-tie to

the left. Cast to the right end of the dock, reel slowly and the lure will run left under the dock overhang, into the shady area where the fish hang out. For the left side of a dock, bend the tie-line to the right. A surface lure with a lip will respond the same way.

Gene Round
Ocala, FL

Double-Purpose Ivory Soap

If you are fishing a trotline and run out of bait, having a large bar of Ivory soap on hand could pay off. Cut chunks of the soap large enough to cover the hook.

And, of course, you can use the soap to wash up after a dirty, smelly day of fishing.

Rodney Campbell
Murphy, NC

Common-Scents Recipe

Here's how to make an inexpensive scent for all of your baits. It is a recipe for success.

2 teaspoons flaked tropical fish food
2 teaspoons pond fish food (pellets)
1 teaspoon salt
1½ teaspoons sugar
1 teaspoon Berkley Power Bait (choose formula designed for the species you are after)
2 teaspoons water
1 sandwich-size zip-top storage bag

Grind up the tropical fish food into little pieces. Dump the ground tropical fish food, pond fish food, salt, sugar and Power Bait attractant into the storage bag. Mix well. Add water. Put bait that you plan to use in the bag and let sit overnight.

Ryan McGrail
Oak Forest, IL

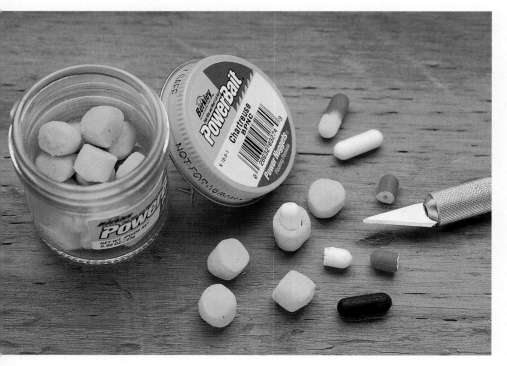

For Maximum Power-Bait Flotation

To give maximum flotation to your Power Bait, insert a small piece of foam-plastic into the middle of your bait before you put the Power Bait on your hook.

Gerald S. Davis
Milanville, PA

Pulley System for Bass

I'm a fisherwoman who loves the excitement of bass tournaments. I have been fishing seriously for about 3 years, and I have discovered that the most important rule to success is being ready when the fish hits.

When fishing with plastic worms on the bottom, I slowly take my left hand and pull my line up 5 or 6 inches, then lower it at a steady pace. I seem to feel the fish a lot easier, and I hook the fish instinctively.

Donna Bennett
Austin, TX

Polish Protects More than Nails

Clear fingernail polish helps protect jig heads, spinnerbait heads and painted spinnerbait blades.

Jeffrey J. Knight
Fayetteville, NC

Fight Pellets with Pellets

When pond fish get accustomed to eating the pellets that they are fed, they may begin to turn up their nose at traditional baits. Try tricking them by wrapping six to ten pellets in old panty hose or netting material found in a crafts store. Simply pile them in a small section of material, wrap them up and tie the material together with sewing thread. This is deadly, for instance, fished under a bobber for catfish.

Jeff Grzeskowiak
Marysville, OH

Double Your Hooking Potential

When fish are picking up plastic worms but not getting hooked, add a trailer hook to your worm hook. Rig the worm Texas style, but before you bury the hook point in the worm, put the trailer hook over the point of the first hook and embed both into the worm.

The addition of the trailer hook doubles your chances of sticking your fish.

B. Nye
Santa Margarita, CA

Two-Worm Rig

Most bass fishermen know there are times when the fishing just shuts down. Then is the time to appeal to the bass's curiosity, and this two-worm rig just might irk him into hitting.

What you will need are two barrel swivels and two worm hooks. I like size 2/0 hooks, but size is your preference. Start by tying one of the hooks to 1 foot of line. Then tie one of the swivels to the end of the 1-foot length.

Next, tie the other hook to a 1½-foot length of line, then tie the other swivel to the end of this line.

Now, thread the line from your reel through the swivel of the shorter of the two lines. Then tie the main line to the swivel of the longer line.

Use this rig with a jerkbait presentation—and hold on!

Douglas Hawley
East Longmeadow, MA

New Look for Spinnerbaits

To create a distinctive flash with your spinnerbait, place strips of masking tape on the blades in various designs. Then paint the blades white or chartreuse. After the paint has dried remove the tape, and your bait will offer a different flash than before.

Leslie J. Richardson
San Benito, TX

Straw Vote

My brother taught me that a ¼-inch piece of plastic straw could simplify my fly tying.

When preparing to build a fly head, whip finish and cement the head, slice the straw segment down the middle, then slip the straw around your tying thread (still on the bobbin) and slide it up and over the hook eye onto the fly. Completely clear any hackle or other materials that may get in the way of a good whip-finish. This works particularly well with dry flies of all sizes.

Alan Vormelker
Cleveland, OH

≈ ADVICE FROM THE PROS ≈

Hooking Bass

When you detect a strike while fishing a crankbait, never set the hook hard. Bass often sideswipe these lures and hook themselves very lightly, and a hard hookset will often rip the hook free. Instead, sweep the rod low and to one side, or simply reel down tight. Treble hooks used on crankbaits today are so sharp, either method will easily bury the barbs.

Don Wirth
Nashville, TN

Improving on a Classic

When fishing a Jitterbug, I have found a way to create even more action when retrieving it. Just bend in the edges of the face plate about ⅛ inch on each end with needle-nose pliers. This will make more of a dish shape and will increase the action.

Leslie J. Richardson
San Benito, TX

Tuna Oil + Garlic = Fish

Save the oil from cans of tuna fish, and mix it with minced garlic and/or garlic-flavored oil. Soak your plastic lures overnight and be prepared to catch fish the next day.

William Picking
Monson, MA

Recondition Your Spinnerbaits

When a spinnerbait blade gets tarnished or rusty, it will not do what it is designed to do. A piece of very fine steel wool will clean those tarnished blades. Rub gently to restore the shine.

Leslie J. Richardson
San Benito, TX

Miracles with Markers

To customize your soft-plastic baiter, use permanent marker of any color to add dots, streaks, etc. Marker does not wash off, but it does wipe off, so you can change colors or patterns (some shadow stain remains).

To spice up lures, use red permanent marker or red paint around the gill area.

To ensure that your ceramic rod guides have no cracks in them, use a washable marker. The marker seeps into cracks, and you can see cracks with ease after you wipe off the excess marker with a damp cloth.

Casey Spranger
Fort Wayne, IN

Colors for Clear and Cloudy Days

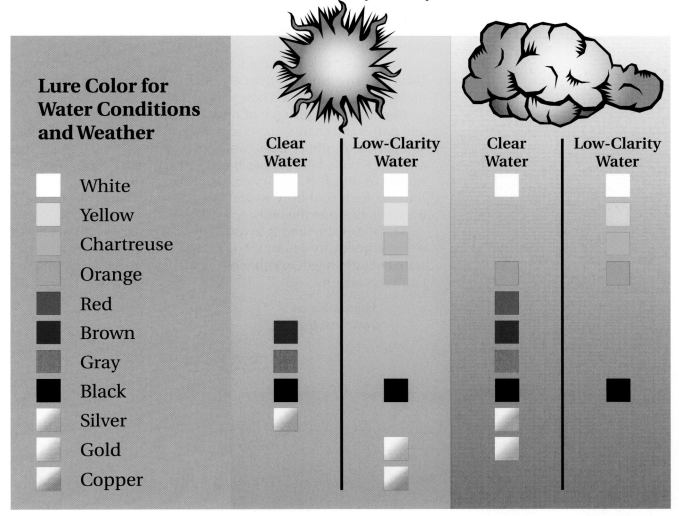

Lure Color for Water Conditions and Weather

	Clear Water	Low-Clarity Water	Clear Water	Low-Clarity Water
White	■	■	■	■
Yellow		■		■
Chartreuse		■	■	■
Orange		■	■	■
Red			■	
Brown	■		■	
Gray	■		■	
Black	■	■	■	■
Silver	■			
Gold		■	■	
Copper		■		

Andy Schneider
Carmel, IN

Free-A-Ma-Jig

Glue, peg or crimp, as I do, a small snap swivel onto one end of a 1-ounce egg sinker. When a crappie hangs up on a branch or limb, attach the snap swivel to the fishing line and drop the sinker straight down to the snag on a tight line. Pop the rod a time or two, if necessary, to free the jig.

Patrick Richter
Dayton, OH

Gee, Whiz

Buy a can of Cheese Whiz or a similar pressurized soft-cheese product. The next time you use a tubebait, fill it up with cheese.

William Picking
Monson, MA

Add Flies to Crappie Jigs

When using jigs for crappies I find it advantageous to add two trailer flies about 6 to 8 inches behind the jig. I suggest you tie the flies on No. 4 or No. 6 hooks on a fine leader.

Leslie J. Richardson
San Benito, TX

Tuning Topwater Baits

Everyone knows that crankbaits, spinnerbaits, even plastic worm-jig combos occasionally need a tune-up. So do topwater baits.

Have you ever watched a frog float or a shad die at the surface? Usually a small part is actually out of the water and the rest is under the surface. That's how your lures should rest in the water.

Depending on the type of topwater bait you are using, you can add rattles and small weights in many ways and places. The hollow soft plastic or rubber frogs can have weights pushed into the legs and body. With solid rubber baits, you can push weights into the rubber or attach it to the hook. With hard-bodied lures, you can drill the body and bury weights, or you can attach weight to the hooks or glue it to the body.

My favorite method is to use Storm SuspenDots. You may need to experiment to determine how much weight works best. You want enough weight to enhance the lure, but not so much that you hinder its action.

Mark Johnson
Tiskilwa, IL

Modify Plugs with Spinners

When casting or trolling medium or large plugs, place a small spinner in front of the plug or remove rear trebles and replace them with a snap and small spinner blade.

Robert Griffiths
Washago, Ontario,
Canada

Carolina Tube-Lure Rig

An effective Carolina rig with a tube lure can be made by inserting a float in the tube lure, which holds the bait above the submerged grass.

Jacob Sheehan
Eastford, CT

Bluegills on Flies

In the early spring, large bluegills like to lie in the shallows and can many times be caught by casting small bass bugs with a fly rod. Small nymphs and dry flies also work well. When fishing shorelines and calm water, make sure you work them slowly, for panfish often look them over well in these types of conditions. You should gently twitch the fly on the retrieve and wait a half-second before setting the hook.

Steve vonBrandt
Wilmington, DE

≋ ADVICE FROM THE PROS ≋

Size Can Make the Difference

Most artificial-lure anglers have a half-dozen pet lures that catch most of the fish in their area. When fish aren't hitting any one of these favorites, they change to another color or lure. The wiser ones carry a range of sizes in each color lure, from ¼ ounce through ⅝ ounce. A change in size often is the key to catching because forage fish hatches come on all year. It's a case of "matching the hatch," and when you offer the conforming size, you can catch a limit quickly.

Gene Round
Ocala, FL

Commons Scents

To keep attracting scent on your bait and not in the air, spray the scent on a sponge in a zip-top plastic bag. The attractant will last longer and give you more use.

Amie Bergmen
Franklin Park, IL

Backward Sliding Sinker

When Texas-rigging a soft-plastic bait, put the bullet weight on backward. This way, when fished on dirt or sand bottoms, the weight will kick up the dirt and possibly attract the fish.

Jimmy Sampson
Huntsville, AL

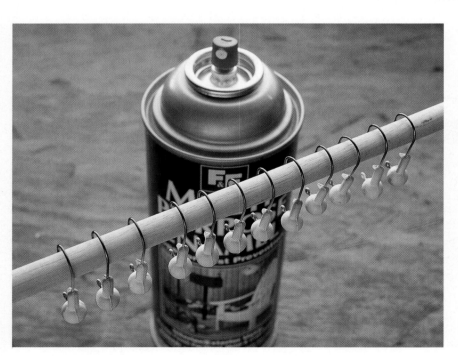

Painting Jig Heads

Hang jig heads from their hooks on a wooden dowel. Hold them up and spray paint them, then turn and paint the other side.

Also, a nut pick makes a great tool for cleaning painted eyelets.

Karl Ulmer
Hawley, PA

Plastic Worm Scents

Here's a great way to make a long-lasting, scent-releasing plastic worm. First, get a 4- to 8-inch plastic worm, a toothpick, a cotton ball, a small straw and a pair of scissors. Then cut a piece of the straw about 1½ inches long. Next pack some of the cotton ball into the small piece of the straw. Now insert the larger part of the unused straw into the end of the worm and bore a hole. After you have a hole about the size of the little straw with cotton, take the large straw out and jam the little straw in. Make sure it is a good, tight fit. Finally, soak the cotton with your favorite scent. I came up with this unique scented worm because every plastic bait I used lost its scent after a while. With this worm, you can replace the scent whenever you want and add as much as you want. It will surely attract more fish. It's just up to you to land them all.

Ryan Zajdzinski
Mokena, IL

Toothpick Tip

To keep an insert such as a rattle or scent-soaked cotton ball in a tubebait, stick a toothpick in one side of the tube, through the insert and out the other side of the tube. Clip or break off the excess toothpick.

Patrick Richter
Dayton, OH

Oh, No, Cod-Liver Oil

When fishing with plastic worms or other soft-plastic bait, spray on or inject them with cod-liver oil, available at most drugstores. You can even use it on spoons and plugs. See if this isn't the remedy for an anemic strike rate.

Robert Griffiths
Washago, Ontario, Canada

More Flash to Buzzbaits

To give your buzzbaits even more flash, cut small ovals from pieces of prism or reflective tape. Place one oval on each blade wing.

Michael Baer
Hazard, KY

Cast Tubebaits Farther

A great way to weigh down your tubebait (to get the extra casting distance sometimes needed) is to rig it up like any other tubebait but take a few BBs and industrial-glue them together. Then put some glue on the end of the BBs and drop them down to the top of the tubebait. I haven't lost any BBs out of the end, and I have found that it creates a great dipping motion that drives spawning bass wild.

Jacob Chavez
Hyannis, MA

Making a Case for Spinnerbaits

At a recent trade show I received a free CD-ROM travel case as a promotional giveaway. Afterward, I found that I had more use for it than I had first thought. I now use it to store my spinnerbaits.

The cases have 24 holder sleeves, and they are clear plastic. This allows me to store my spinnerbaits simply and tangle free. I also can see the skirt color and blade type of the bait before getting it out. I keep two cases in my big tackle box and have my spinnerbaits roughly divided into dark and light. If I desire, I can grab just my spinnerbaits, throw them into a jacket pocket and stroll down to the water with a good selection of baits in a tangle-free holder without lugging my entire tackle box.

Jim Zaleski
New York, NY

Another Use for WD-40

WD-40 may be manufactured as a lubricant, but after squirting it on a variety of lures when fishing for both freshwater and saltwater species, I am convinced that it is an excellent fish attractant. Don't give up on the commercially made scents, but don't ignore this one. It may work when others aren't getting the job done.

Glenn Sapir
Putnam Valley, NY

No Kiddin'

Try using Preparation H, the hemorrhoidal ointment, as an attractant scent for crappies. It really works.

Patrick Richter
Dayton, OH

Bass on Top

If you are fishing at night, here are a couple of tips: During early to mid spring when the water temperature is 55 to 60°F, I like to use a lot of surface lures. Cast into inlets and along cover. Remember that some of the hottest times for topwater baits are during spring.

During early to mid-summer, on bright nights, I like to use a spinnerbait with a single Colorado blade. I cast into dark areas near cover. Big bass hide in the shadow of these dark areas and dart out to catch bugs and baitfish, then retreat back to the shadows. It is always good to have night spinners with large Colorado blades in your tackle box.

Richard Fridley
Indianola, IA

Removable Texas Rig

One of my favorite and most productive lures is a Texas-rigged plastic worm. Often, however, I want to change to other types of lures. Instead of tying and retying my Texas rig each time I want to go back to it, I simply snell a 12- to 20-inch length of monofilament to my worm hook, slip on a bullet weight and then tie a loop at the end. Now I can tie a snap or snap-swivel to my line and change to and from lures within seconds.

Chad Falls
Via e-mail

Light Up Your Tubebaits

Insert a small cyalume lightstick into the back of a tubebait. If necessary, wedge a toothpick next to the lightstick to help keep it in place.

Add a minnow to the bait, and you have one of my favorite nighttime fishing jigs for walleye. I prefer clear or green tubes, but don't be afraid to experiment.

Matt Radzialowski
Wixom, MI

Salvage Plastic Worms

Don't just toss away plastic worms with split heads. Cut off small lengths and try them on panfish.

Nick Layman
Via e-mail

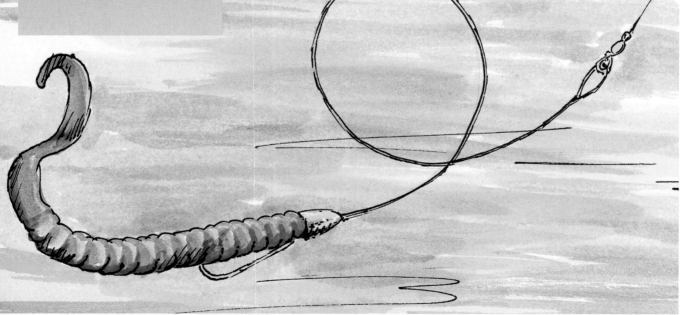

Cut Hook, Cut Snags

Cutting off the forward hook of the front treble on a crankbait greatly reduces snags. It also reduces lure loss, yet does not reduce fish catch rate.

Alan Meeker
Columbia, MO

Prime Time for Dry Flies

There are two times in the day when you can catch panfish, and even bass, by using a dry fly. The times are when the sun starts to come up so there is just enough light to see the fly, and just before sundown, when you can barely see your fly skimming the top of the water from the shore.

Jon Hellmers
Shakopee, MN

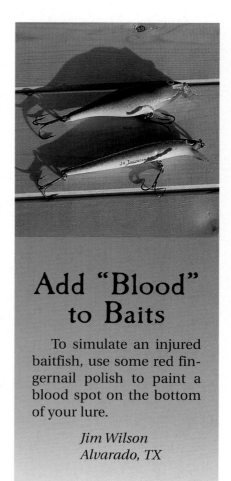

Spinner-Minnow Lure Combo

I have found that attaching a small spinner to a small minnow-type plug can be very effective on trout in streams and rivers. The added flash and action triggers strikes when other lures fail.

Josh Estep
Elizabethton, TN

Add "Blood" to Baits

To simulate an injured baitfish, use some red fingernail polish to paint a blood spot on the bottom of your lure.

Jim Wilson
Alvarado, TX

ARTIFICIAL BAIT

Fish with a Fizz

I use Alka Seltzer in some baits! You just break one tablet in two and put one half into a tubebait. This fizz excites the fish.

Jacob Kline
Benton Harbor, MI

Scent Your Worms

When you buy new plastic worms that have no scent, put them in a container. Then pour in salt or any other spices such as garlic or onion salts. This will give the worms a strong scent and flavor that the big fish cannot resist.

Josh Grabow
Crescent City, IL

Securing Jig Tails

Heat the collar of an unpainted jig head before sliding on the plastic tail. The heat melts the plastic, and when it cools and hardens, it adheres to the head. This prevents the tail from slipping back off the collar when a fish grabs it, or when you set the hook hard and miss. This action will save you time and money, and it is simple.

Ryan Zajdzinski
Mokena, IL

Add Rattle to Tubebaits

For more sound when tube-bait fishing, insert two glass rattles (available from tackle shops and catalogs) into the tube, then Texas-rig the bait so that the hook holds the rattles in place.

Michael Baer
Hazard, KY

Worms for Pike and Muskie

Though it's true that the plastic worm was designed for bass fishing, it can be a deadly pike and muskie lure. One reason is because plastic worms are seldom used, and these battlers aren't used to seeing them. Also, they can be rigged weedless and go where pike and muskie lures get hung up. Try this:

Texas-rig a 12-inch giant weed-less, one with a flat, curly tail. Reel it very s-l-o-w-l-y over weeds, lily pads, brush and around fallen timber. The explosive strikes this ignites will not only add a special glow to your day, but the big average size of the fish you catch will astound your fishing buddies. Take along a few extra giant worms for them; they'll be wanting some!

Gene Round
Ocala, FL

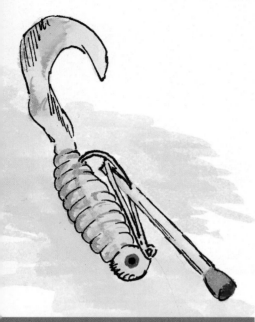

Jig Made Weedless

I buy small rubber bands used for braces from an orthodontist. I loop this rubber band over a jig head under the eye and stretch the other end of the band under the hook, around the hook end, and then seat it into the hook barb notch. I use a heavy toothpick, wooden matchstick or small tweezers to facilitate seating the rubber band into the barb notch. Weeds tend to slide off the jig, but a fish bite easily dislodges the rubber band.

Ronald C. Dobrunz
Davis, IL

New Bass Rigs for Tough Times

There are days when you can beat the water to a froth without ever getting bit. You try downsizing, going deep, going shallow, looking for suspended bass—all to no avail. On days like this, make unorthodox rigs the bass have never seen. I've had success using strange combinations of lures when nothing else would tempt Mr. Bass. Here are a few combinations that gave me an edge:

Tie on a small crankbait (2½ to 3 inches). Remove the rear hook. Add a swivel or split ring and a larger (6- to 9-inch) shallow running bait about 3 to 4 inches behind the small bait. The combination gives two different actions with two separate vibrations. The overall appearance resembles a small predator chasing a baitfish. This can bring out reaction strikes from competitive bass.

Don't throw away old buzzbait blades. These can be used in combination with many standard lures. You need to replace the existing wire that runs through the blade with a short piece of wire and a swivel or split ring. Attach the blade ahead of minnowbaits, lipless crankbaits or anything else you want to try. One of the best combinations I've found is to add 12 to 18 inches of line with a Texas-rigged worm or soft jerk or tubebait. Fish this rig with a stop-and-go retrieve. The buzzbait blade will draw their attention during the retrieve. When stopped, the plastic free-falls behind the slowly sinking blade. This rig has proven very effective in clear water and over weedbeds or rocks.

Try using topwater baits on the bottom. Just add a weight that will sink the lure. Zara Spooks, Jitterbugs, Heddon Tiny Torpedoes and Pop-Rs are seldom seen 8 to 10 feet below the surface, and bass may react in your favor.

Jointed minnow-type or shallow crankbaits can be used in combination with worms, grubs, tubes and other parts of jointed minnow-type baits. Replace the rear hook with a split ring on the crankbait and add your choice to the connecting eye. On jointed minnows, keep the front half of the minnow lure intact and add something different behind. One time while trolling for stripers, I added split rings, treble hooks and two tail sections to a jointed Rebel. This foot-long monster scored. No one else got a strike, but the long Rebel caught two nice stripers.

Use your imagination and try anything you want. When nothing else works, you don't have much to lose. You may develop a combination that produces fish on those extremely tough days. The right combination might even warrant commercial interest and help finance your fishing.

William L. McCabe
Napa, CA

Two-Color Jig Heads

Use bicolor jig heads to increase your odds of offering the right color. Fish can be very picky, and that's why these babies are great! It's amazing that something so simple can work so well. You can buy them or make your own by taping half the head, then dipping them in fluorescent paint. This will improve the number of fish you catch because you are offering a variety.

Ryan Zajdzinski
Mokena, IL

Fattening Frogs and Rats

It takes a powerful rod and heavy line to horse a big largemouth out of lily pads or matted surface hydrilla. Unfortunately, it's hard to cast one of the most effective styles of weedless lure, the hollow soft-plastic frog or rat, on such heavy tackle. For greater casting distance without sacrificing the lure's flotation, cut a small slit in the back of the bait and cram the hollow body cavity full of pinched-off pieces of plastic worm. While you're at it, add a couple of glass worm rattles to help bass hone in on your rat or frog in thick surface vegetation.

Don Wirth
Nashville, TN

Knot Placement Matters

Tie on a minnow plug with a knot that clinches tightly to the attachment eye. Slide the knot toward the bottom of the eye for the most wiggle. This will increase strikes and catch more fish.

Ryan Zajdzinski
Mokena, IL

Short-Strike Remedy

Are you bothered by short strikes on your favorite Johnson weedless spoon/pork rind combination? Don't fear, ingenuity can remedy the problem.

Using a quality snap swivel, slide the swivel over your hook and up to the spoon body. Secure the swivel in place with a small amount of J. B. Weld. You may have to bend the swivel slightly to make it line up with the spoon body, but it won't affect the swivel or the action of the spoon.

Now you have an easy-access snap to add your own trailers, such as large flies or a weedless single hook with a twister tail.

Rex Ballard
Benzonia, MI

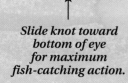

Slide knot toward bottom of eye for maximum fish-catching action.

Paint Your Lures

I want certain color combos on lures that I can't seem to buy, so I have found a way to paint them to meet my changes.

If I wish to have the belly of a lure white, I can change it this way: First, take the blister pack that they come in, open it carefully, and try to just remove the cardboard from the clear blister top. Then remove the hooks from the lure. Cut out a hole in the clear part of the package a little smaller than you wish the area of new color to be.

Then, take a small piece of masking tape, roll it up so it is sticky all the way around and use it to fasten the top of the lure to the cardboard portion of the package. You can see through the clear part to position the lure perfectly under the template painting hole that you cut earlier. Hold or tape the blister pack together and spray over it, being careful to keep the spray can parallel to the package. I usually give it two thin coats rather than risk getting paint runs.

With a little care, this will feather the paint nicely and give it a factory look.

John F. Toews
Omaha, NE

ADVICE FROM THE PROS

Pruning Your Pork

Modifying your pork trailers can increase their action for a more effective presentation. If bass are striking deep, trim some of the fat from the head of the pork so your jig or spinnerbait will fall faster. If you're not getting bites, try cutting several small notches in the legs to make them more wiggly.

Don Wirth
Nashville, TN

Add Sticking Power to Soft Plastics

When fishing with soft plastics, I have found that short strikes tend to pull off the worm, grub or whatever bait I am using. This discourages second strikes, of course.

To reduce the problem, I now squeeze a small amount of industrial-strength glue onto the shank of the hook and the bottom of the head of a jig. Not only does this allow me to hook more fish, but it saves me money by not having to replace so many baits.

Chad Lukehart
Vale, OR

Tubebait Touch-Ups

I fish tubes a lot, sometimes putting foam or rattles in them. Sometimes the rattles or foam don't fit very well, so I developed a way to keep them in place. First, I find a plastic worm that is similar in color to the tube and will fit into it well. Then, with the foam or rattle in place, I take a lighter and melt the worm, quickly sticking the worm into the tube and trimming off the excess. It makes a clean, seamless plug in the tube. You can experiment with different-colored worms and leave the worm sticking out of the tube for a combination of worm and tube. You can also make the tube float by sealing air in the tube.

Sean P. Conroy
Spooner, WI

Buzzbait Booster

An effective way to increase strikes on buzzbaits is to add a trailer hook rigged with a soft-plastic grub. As you run the buzzer across the surface, stop every so often and let it sink a little. Then re-start your surface retrieve. You'll be amazed at the number of hits you get. Most of the fish I catch hit the buzzbait after I stop the retrieve, then let it sink, or right after I re-start it, just before it breaks the surface.

Mark S. Copeland
Winamac, IN

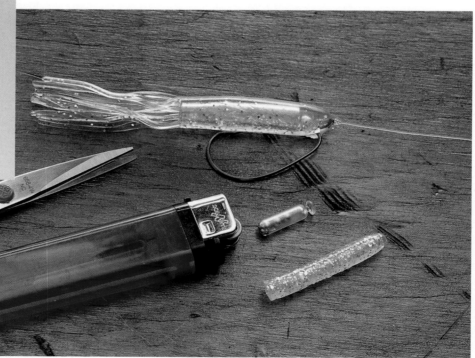

Making Spoons More Weedless

Make a spoon even more weedless by pushing a plastic worm onto the weed guard. Bend the hook slightly outward so that it will penetrate the worm. Try to use a color worm that contrasts with the color of the spoon. The combination of the worm and the different colors is sure to catch you more fish in that heavy cover, while preventing the spoon from snagging.

Ryan Zajdzinski
Mokena, IL

≈ ADVICE FROM THE PROS ≈

Spinnerbait Advice in Depth

How deep should you retrieve a spinnerbait? A good rule of thumb is to keep the lure moving at a speed where you can just barely see the blades flashing. In murky water, this would keep the lure within a foot or so of the surface, while in clear water, the lure would be considerably deeper.

Don Wirth
Nashville, TN

Big Fish/ Small Fish Rig

I primarily fish for walleye and bass using an artificial—usually a Rattle-trap or other crankbait. But I also like to catch bluegills, crappies and perch. So, I tie an 18-inch piece of 6- or 8-pound test with a Uni Knot onto my main line, 10-pound test. I leave about 6 inches on the short end, a foot on the long end. This leaves a dropper line a foot or so above the crankbait, and onto it I'll tie a size 8 or 10 jig with a small twister tail. This way, while fishing for big species with the crankbait I can be fishing for panfish with the jig.

Take note, however, that the fish won't read this book and might not follow the rules. In fact, I have a 5-pound bass on the wall that didn't follow the rules; it hit the small jig on the dropper. I have caught bluegills, crappies, perch, carp and even channel cats on this rig.

Clyde King
Tiffin, OH

Half-Lizard Trailer

A half-lizard trailer helped me catch a 9-pound largemouth. I cut a plastic lizard in half and put the rear end on a jig. The new trailer looked ultrarealistic, with two legs and a tail swimming around.

You can experiment with color, but black works best for me.

Jonathan Vinea
Alamo, CA

Treble Hook Fly/Spinner Combo

Steelheaders can really increase their chances of hooking more fish by adding a treble hook fly to their spinner rigs. Here's what you have to do:

First, cut the existing hook from the spinner. Next, attach a split ring to a treble hook fly and to the spinner. It's that simple. You may choose to use scent on the fly.

Jim W. Enbysk
Pendleton, OR

Float Your Tubebait

If bass yawn at your lizard or worm when you drag it past them on a Carolina rig, try floating tubebait instead. Break off a piece from a foam packing peanut and cram it inside the hollow tube to make it float, then insert a light-wire worm hook. When fished on a 2-foot leader behind a heavy Carolina sinker, the tube will dart about like an injured baitfish.

Don Wirth
Nashville, TN

Glitter with Glue

Buy some low-cost glitter glue and apply it to a plain brass or silver spoon. After applying the glue, add some fish scent to the spoon to cover the smell and taste of the glue.

Edward Thompson
Arvada, CO

Lipless Lures

Don't throw away your old floating minnow-type baits when the lips become broken. You can break the lip completely off, sand and/or repaint the lure and use it as a surface lure for bass, pike or any other surface-feeding fish. Just tie it on, cast it out and twitch it erratically across the surface.

Steve vonBrandt
Wilmington, DE

Skirt Support

A good way to keep a skirt on your jig or spinnerbait is to get some heavy nylon thread. Wrap the thread several times around the skirt and hook, then tie a knot. I tie two to three knots, so that the thread does not come untied. This thread will last longer than the rubber bands that come with skirts.

Scott Torbeck
St. Peter, IL

Old sayings get old for a reason: There's usually a lot of truth to them. Here's one old saying that's as true as ever: Your fishing line is your direct and only link to the fish you're trying to catch. If that line is old or frayed or nicked or too thick or too thin or your knots are poor … then goodbye fish (or, maybe worse yet, you might never even get to say hello). Terminal tackle—the rigs you create—is important too.

Take care of your line and terminal tackle, tie good knots that work. If you don't, everything else is for naught.

Removable Sinker

I use snagless sinkers, but many times when fishing I discover I need a different size than the one I have on my rig. Typically, to change sinkers, you have to take everything apart, remove it, then reassemble the whole thing.

However, by cutting the eyelet of a flat-type snagless sinker with pliers, you can take the sinker off the line easily by spreading the eyelet apart. You can easily slip on a different size weight that also has had its eyelet cut. The lead is soft and the cut can be closed with the same pliers.

The whole process takes a minute or two, then the bait is back in the river.

Tom Smiley
Munhall, PA

Straighten Twisted Line

If you are boat fishing with either spinning or bait-casting tackle and you realize that your line has twisted causing kinks, knots and problems wrapping around the rod tip, simply cut off your terminal tackle, so that there is nothing but line. Then slowly let out all of your line while the boat is moving forward. The forward motion of the boat untwists the line as it drags in the water. After pulling the line for 50 yards or so, reel in all of the line. You'll be happy to find a newly straightened spool. This process only takes a few minutes to accomplish.

Cameron Mitchell
Greensboro, NC

Line Diameter Matters

When fishing a popper in choppy water, use a large diameter line. A small diameter line lies deeper in the water, so the chugger dives forward. A larger diameter line will ride the lure higher in the water and make it jump.

Jacob Sheehan
Eastford, CT

Twist-On Sinkers

Next time you are live bait fishing, try using twist-on sinkers instead of split-shot. They can be cut into small pieces for very little weight or doubled up for more weight. They are almost snagless in weeds (good for minnow fishing in weedbeds) when the ends are twisted on tight. They don't pinch your line as split-shot do, and you can untwist them and cut a piece off if you start with too much weight. So far I've caught more fish in tighter places than I could have with split-shot.

Steven Bjonnes
Hanover, PA

Power-Bait Trout Leaders

Plenty of trout fishermen use floating baits with packaged snelled hooks (about 6 inches long) and a slip-sinker. Often, they fish for hours without success. The problem is, the weed growth is 10 to 14 inches on the bottom and their bait is hidden below it. Learn to tie your own leaders in different lengths, from 12 inches to 4 feet long. Start with the shortest and go up until you start catching fish.

William L. McCabe
Napa, CA

Fortify Your Knots

Put a tube of industrial-strength glue, in gel form, in your tackle box. Use a drop on all knots, especially when you are using braided line. It can also be used to repair plastic worms and tubebaits that get torn up.

Ray Kalisz
Battle Creek, MI

Last-Minute Jigs

Don't you hate it when you run out of jigheads or misplace them? This is what you should do when that happens: On any size hook that fits your needs, squeeze a medium-size or larger split-shot just below the hook's eye. You can soften the lead with a cigarette lighter and permanently affix the split-shot. You can also color the split-shot with a permanent marker.

Robert J. Gotschall
Steubenville, OH

Lend Me an Ear(ring)

The "stops" from old earrings can help keep a trailer hook in place. I've tried plastic and rubber tubes, but they hold the hook stiffly and do not allow it to move freely.

Simply put the second hook's eye over the point of the first hook, then slip the earring stop over the first hook's point.

Wayne L. Smead
Minneapolis, MN

Another Fish-Bite Detector

If you're fishing with bait for catfish, walleye, bass or any type of big fish, try my way of detecting that the bait has been picked up.

Take a typical red-and-white round bobber—for weight and to catch your eye—and place a little Christmas jingle bell on one end of the bobber. Attach the other end of the bobber to your line, in between the two bottom guides. You'll hear the bell ring and see the bobber move before the fish has had a chance to get away with your bait.

Robert J. Gotschall
Steubenville, OH

Getting Old Is a Real Sew and Sew

As you get older and your eyesight diminishes, use a needle threader to put fishing line on your hook.

Albert J. Rodzinak
Middlesex, NJ

Line Protector

Are you the type of angler who likes to fish with ultralight line but is afraid to use split-shot sinkers because you are afraid they will weaken or cut your line? If so, try this idea on for size.

When a portable radio, Walkman or kid's toy that runs on batteries breaks, don't be too quick to discard the item. First, look internally for their teeny weeny coated wires. Strip the coatings off the wires and cut these coatings into 1-inch pieces. Keep them in your tackle box.

When you want to use a split-shot, slide a piece of the coating onto your line, then pinch the split-shot onto the coating. These coatings greatly cushion your line and also will grip your line when a split-shot is added.

Milton Donahue
Syracuse, NY

Organized Leaders

You can store long leaders for floating trout baits by using empty cardboard rolls from bathroom tissue. Hold the loop on the tube sideways and wrap the leader around the tube, going over the loop. Pull a little stretch in the leader and set the point of the hook into the tube. It doesn't have to go very deep, just enough to hold. Pull the hook free and unroll your leader when ready to use. You can store pre-tied Carolina rigs using the same technique. Everyone has a constant supply of rolls, and there's something worthwhile to use them for.

William L. McCabe
Napa, CA

Favorite Hook Sharpener

The best hook sharpener I've ever found is an ignition file. It's thin, easy to use and lasts for years.

Jeffrey J. Knight
Fayetteville, NC

Fishing at the Pier

When you decide to go fishing on the pier, determine what is being caught, and what you would like to fish for. You'll need to know which fish inhabit the waters, both seasonally and all year.

In order to catch the right fish, you need to use the right rig at the right time of year. The tackle shops at the pier will be able to tell you what types of fish are being caught, and what type of bait to use.

Baiting a hook is very important, as the bait must cover the hook but not be too large. See the chart below for recommended bait sizes. I prefer a Palomar knot (page 70) over a cinch knot for attaching hooks and swivels.

Always carry an extra rig. I also recommend that you carry a fish identification guide to avoid getting a ticket. A current copy of the fishing regulations is another must for the tackle box.

Last but not least, remember that patience is the most important part of pier fishing!

Marc J. Lawrence
Torrance, CA

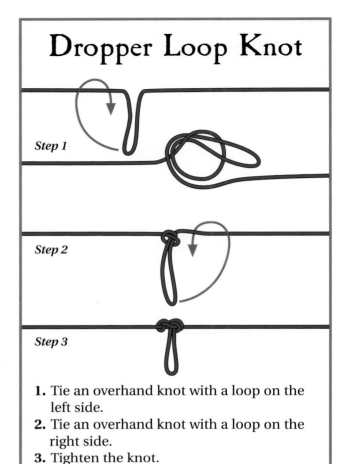

Dropper Loop Knot

Step 1

Step 2

Step 3

1. Tie an overhand knot with a loop on the left side.
2. Tie an overhand knot with a loop on the right side.
3. Tighten the knot.

Recommended Bait for Typical Pier Fish

Smelt—Use squid cut into ¼- x ¼-inch pieces. Smelt have small mouths, so be sure to use small hooks.

Mackerel—Use squid cut into ½- x ½-inch strips. Use No. 2 or No. 4 hooks on a bait rig that can be drifted or weighted to the bottom.

Tom Cod—Use squid on a bait rig.

Queen Fish and Sardines—Use squid on a white fly bait rig. Sardines require a slow yo-yo action.

Perch—Use the tough portion of clams on small hooks, and drift the rig with a float.

Halibut—Use strip bait with a split tail. Move the bait every 5-10 minutes, then stop.

Sharks and Rays—Use fish cut into 1- x 3-inch strips.

Sand Bass—Use live bait when possible.

I catch my own bait by nose-hooking a small fish on a bait rig. Cast out slowly and move every few minutes.

Slip Bait Rig

This works best for halibut and sand bass when using live smelt or other small fish as bait.

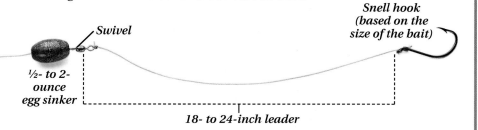

Swivel

Snell hook (based on the size of the bait)

½- to 2-ounce egg sinker

18- to 24-inch leader

Dropper Loop Rig

This works best for sand bass and bay bass with live baitfish.

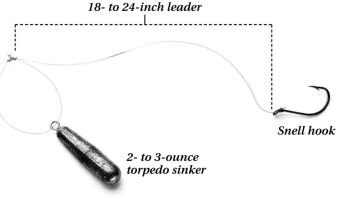

18- to 24-inch leader

Snell hook

2- to 3-ounce torpedo sinker

Bonito Fly Rig

Use a clear surf float, partially filled with water and small shot.

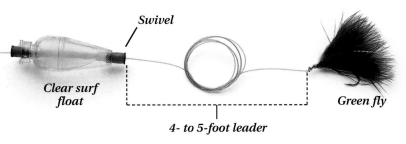

Swivel

Clear surf float

Green fly

4- to 5-foot leader

Smelt Rig (Redondo Style)

Use small pieces of squid when fishing for smelt. These fish have small mouths.

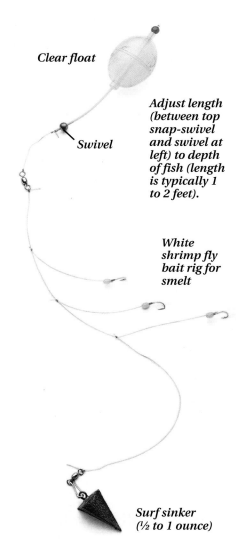

Snap-swivel above float (not shown)

Clear float

Swivel

Adjust length (between top snap-swivel and swivel at left) to depth of fish (length is typically 1 to 2 feet).

White shrimp fly bait rig for smelt

Surf sinker (½ to 1 ounce)

Editor's Note: All the rigs and information on pages 64–67 were provided by member Marc J. Lawrence from Torrance, California. Thanks for the great pier-fishing info, Marc!

Slider-Bait Rig

This rig works well on sharks. Use fish strips for bait.

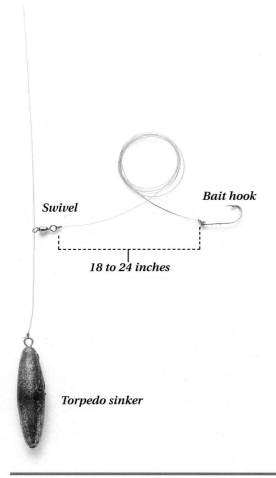

Swivel

Bait hook

18 to 24 inches

Torpedo sinker

Fish-Finder Rig

This works best with two different bait types. Drop it to the bottom, then bring it up one reel-handle turn.

3-foot leader

Torpedo sinker

Santa Monica Perch Rig

This works best when mussels are wrapped around the hook.

Surf float

Swivel

Treble hook

Pismo Beach Pier Bait Rig

This is a white shrimp fly rig used to catch bait such as perch and smelt.

Pre-Tied Surf Rig

Use anchovy and squid for rays and skates. Use clams for perch.

Mackerel Rig

Use pieces of squid for bait to get mackerel. Adjust the depth of the rig to the fish's location.

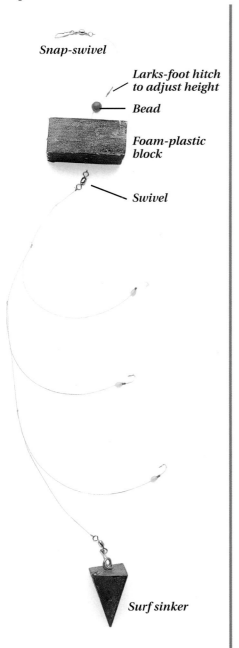

Snap-swivel

Larks-foot hitch to adjust height

Bead

Foam-plastic block

Swivel

Surf sinker

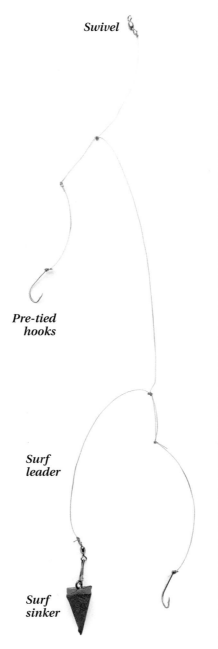

Swivel

Pre-tied hooks

Surf leader

Surf sinker

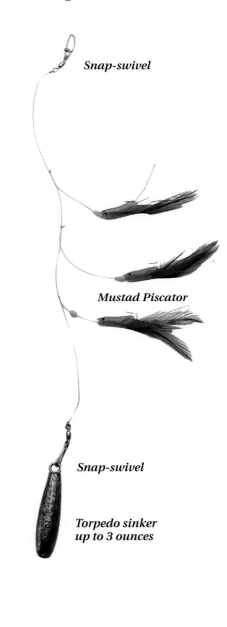

Snap-swivel

Mustad Piscator

Snap-swivel

Torpedo sinker up to 3 ounces

Editor's Note: All the rigs and information on pages 64–67 were provided by member Marc J. Lawrence from Torrance, California. Thanks for the great pier-fishing info, Marc!

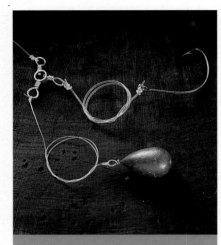

River Rig

River rigs are made by using a 3-way swivel and then adding 12 to 18 inches of monofilament leader to your hook and a dropper off one of the other line ties. I make my droppers out of old, lightweight mono with a loop knot at the end. I attach the sinker by passing the loop through the sinker eye, and then I bring the loop back over the sinker. That way I can change sinkers without tying a new knot, and the light mono allows me to lose just the sinker if I get caught in a snag.

Joel Schollmeier
Prescott, WI

Egg-Loop Tie

Steelheaders and salmon fishermen know the advantages of fishing with yarn. Besides attracting the fish, it gets into the fish's teeth while it is biting, giving you more time to set the hook. Here's an effective way to make an "egg-loop tie" and a "yarn-egg-loop tie."

EGG-LOOP TIE

1. Place hook in vise; cut piece of leader 24 inches long.

2. Insert one end of leader through eye and down shank of hook, about 1 to 1½ inches past end of hook. Hold leader in place with left thumb and forefinger near base of hook eye.

3. With right thumb/forefinger, take leader and wrap around hook eye, toward yourself, six to eight wraps around the shank of the hook, starting at base of eye and working toward back of hook. Do not overlap wraps.

4. With right hand, slide right thumb/forefinger down line about 2 inches and hold.

5. With left hand, take end of leader and place on top of hook shank and run end of line through end of hook, about 1 to 1½ inches. Continue to hold line in place.

6. With right thumb/forefinger, continue to make six to eight wraps on shank of hook, wrapping toward you.

7. After wrapping, take right hand and pull leader down tight and hold.

8. Slightly wet thumb and forefinger of left hand and run them over line to be pulled through wraps. Moistening line allows it to pull through without fraying.

9. Change position of left hand with right.

10. With right hand, pull end of line protruding through eye until line is tight.

Yarn-Egg-Loop Tie

1. Double a piece of single-strand yarn, cut to size you want (normally length of hook or shorter).

2. Open egg-loop tie on hook, tie yarn on center of egg-loop leader, pull tight. Trim excess.

Jim Enbysk
Pendleton, OR

Save on Slip-Sinkers

One way to save some money is to buy unpainted bullet weights in bulk (100) from mail-order companies. Buying packages of painted weights at the local tackle shop can really hurt your wallet, so I take these bulk packs and paint them myself.

I use a toothpick to hold an individual bullet weight and then, using a small brush, I paint the weight with Testor's (normally black) model paint. I have found this paint to be very good for this application because it goes on smoothly and only takes one coat. After the weight is painted, I insert the other end of the toothpick into a piece of Styrofoam for drying, then repeat those steps with the other weights. After all the weights are dry (1 to 2 hours), I then paint on one coat of premium rod varnish to put a protective coating on the paint. If painted this way, the paint job on these bullet weights lasts a long time (much longer than retail bullet weights) and costs considerably less.

Jim Meredith
Lakeland, FL

No More Mess

I like to use Blakemore Reel and Line Magic, but I had trouble with the mess when sprayed. I solved this by using the red straw from a bottle of WD-40. The straw fits perfectly into the nozzle, and the spray can be controlled very precisely.

Jeffrey J. Knight
Fayetteville, NC

Thumbnail Sketch of Sharpness

A way to see if your hook is sharp is to pull it along your thumbnail. If it catches on the nail, your hook is sharp. If it doesn't, it means your hook needs some sharpening.

Jason Hilton
Telford, TN

Check Nicks and Knots

Always check your line for little nicks or knots because the smallest nick can cost you a large fish. I was fishing in Maine and was getting laughed at for retying my knots. That changed when I was the only one who landed big fish (others hooked, but lost them).

Jacob Depot
Ledyard, CT

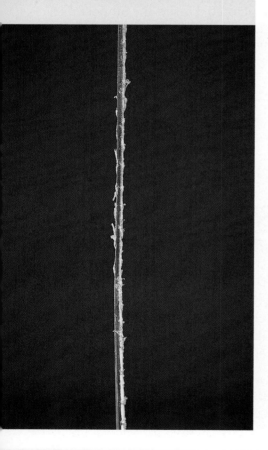

Palomar Knot

1. Thread a 6-inch loop of line through the hook eye.

2. Tie an overhand knot.

3. Take the loop over the hook.

4. Pull tight and clip off tag end.

Marc Lawrence
Torrance, CA

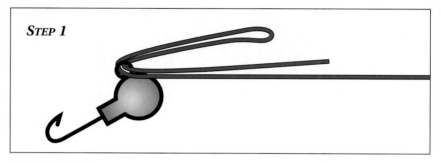

STEP 1

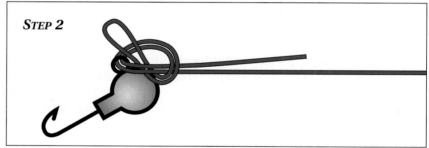

STEP 2

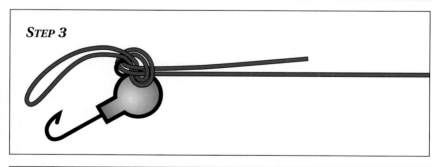

STEP 3

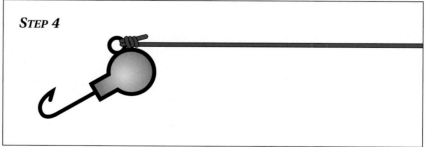

STEP 4

Close Those Clips

I use a lot of snap-swivels, and I finally came to realize that if I didn't snap them closed in storage, I would come up with a tangle of them the next time I went to my tackle box. Now, I make sure that they are all snapped, and when I go for one, that's all I get.

The same is true, of course, for clip-type stringers. When you take fish off the stringer at the end of the day, wash down the stringer and close those clips. It will save you from encountering a nightmarish tangle the next time you want to use the stringer.

Javad Trew
Petaluma, CA

Versatile Circle Hooks

Circle hooks are not just for live bait fishing. I've caught smallmouth bass on a tubebait rigged with a circle hook and carp with dough balls on a circle hook. Almost always the fish is hooked on the corner of the mouth, making release safe and easy.

Patrick Richter
Dayton, OH

≋ ADVICE FROM THE PROS ≋

Bobberology

Bobber reading is an art, and those thus skilled catch more panfish than tightliners. Add enough pinch-on sinkers to sink all but the tip of the bobber. Paint the bobber tip bright red and observe it closely. If the bobber tilts right or left, a panfish has taken the bait from the opposite side. Set the hook! If the bobber disappears suddenly, a panfish is going home with the bait. Set the hook … and grin!

Gene Round
Ocala, FL

Carolina Rig Timesaver

To save time with Carolina rigging, pre-tie hooks and swivels onto leaders. These leaders store neatly on empty line spools.

Jeffery J. Knight
Fayetteville, NC

Marshmallow Bobbers

If you fish for trout in lakes and streams that are filled with moss, then you are probably aware of the problem with your bait sinking into the greenery, where the fish don't see it; each time you bring in the line, you have to clean it off.

Miniature marshmallows float and when used with bait will keep it off the bottom where the fish can see it. A marshmallow alone can catch trout, but it's even more effective when corn, nightcrawlers or salmon eggs are added.

Always put the marshmallow on first. I like to squeeze it flat and put a bait-holder hook through the middle. Then I run the marshmallow up the line and out of the way, and then add the bait. Then I slide the marshmallow back down over the knot and eye of the hook.

Steve vonBrandt
Wilmington, DE

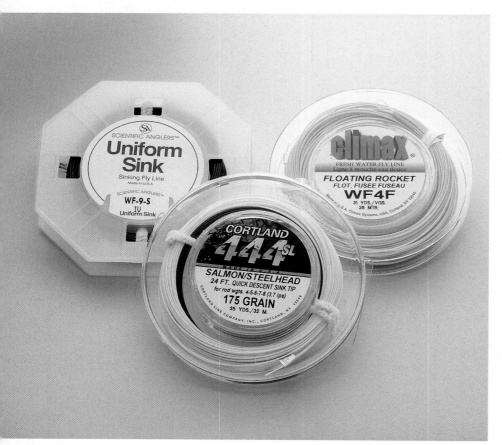

Line-Changing Advice

Since I do a lot of fishing, I change my line often. To save money on the ever-increasing price of quality line I use a backing of less expensive line, which I purchase in bulk spools. Filling the spool to a little more than half its capacity, then joining a more expensive line of my choice with a Uni Knot, I have yet to have a bass spool me to the knot. This tip is not suggested, however, for stripers, big cats or off-shore angling.

When I do change my line I use a wooden dowel and a power drill to remove the line. Usually one dowel will last for an entire season.

Karl Ulmer
Hawley, PA

Lose Split-Shot, Not Lures

When fishing streams, rivers or bodies of water with rocky bottoms, I leave a tag end of about a foot or two where I tie my line onto the lure or bait. Attach split-shot to the tag end for weight. If a hang up occurs while fishing rocky-bottom waters, the weights will hang up and slip off the tag end of the line and I usually can free my bait or lure with a sharp snap of the rod.

Chris Winter
Via e-mail

Cork to Straighten Line

A cork from a wine bottle can help straighten twisted monofilament. With a razor, cut the cork from top to bottom on an angle from the side to the middle, stopping at the midway point. Now simply let the twisted line pay off your reel, slip the line through the slit in the cork just beyond your tiptop and reel in the line, through the cork.

Ross Gough
Key West, FL

Pen Springs Help Hooking

Save the springs from your ballpoint pens to wrap on your favorite hooks to improve the baiting of dough baits, cheese baits, etc.

Dennis Malkin
Gates Mills, OH

Whisper-Light Slip Bobber

Here's a way that you can make dandy little whisper-light slip bobbers. Start with a small plastic tube that comes taped to a can of WD-40. Drill a tiny hole through a cork. Cut the plastic tube about ⅛ inch longer than the cork. You can use sandpaper to shape your cork any way you'd like; I shape mine like a walnut. Insert the plastic tube through the cork, so that about ⅙ inch sticks out on each end. Dab a little nail polish where the tube emerges from the cork to lock the tube in place.

Milton Donahue
Syracuse, NY

Line to Lead-Core Connection

When you want to join monofilament line to lead-core Dacron, don't use a swivel; it can hang up in the tiptop of your rod and the line guide of your trolling reel. An old-timer taught me a great alternative.

First, tie four loose half-hitches about a foot up the lead-core line. Leave the knots open about 1 inch.

Next, pinch the lead core with your fingernails, then slide the outer Dacron sheath back about 3 inches. Cut off those 3 inches of lead core.

Then, take the monofilament and insert it into the Dacron sheath. Carefully work it into the sheath while slipping the sheath over the monofilament until you have the 3 inches of monofilament inside the sheath and you feel it "bottom out" against the lead core.

Now, pinch the end of the sheath to prevent the mono from coming out and work the first half-hitch knot down to the end of the outer sheath and pull it snug. Move the rest of the half-hitch knots down as close as you can get them to the first knot and pull them snug. Done correctly, you will have four half-hitch knots within the first half-inch of Dacron.

You can pull all you want on this knot, and it will not slip or loosen before you overstress and break the line.

Milt Jacobson
Post Falls, ID

Lure Desnagger

An easy gadget that will help you limit your losses of lures due to snags is made by putting a heavy bell sinker on a snap-swivel. To use it, snap the swivel over your line and let the weight pull it down to your lure. Then shake your rod a few times, and the lure should come free.

Jimmy Sampson
Huntsville, AL

Reversal of Color

Some of the best fishing in my area occurs where I have to row to earn my trout. The preferred method is to get your lure down to the fish by employing lead-core line, about 5 feet of depth earned for every 25 feet of line let out. To let you know how deep you might be, the manufacturers of the lead core provide a new color for every 25 or 30 feet of line.

If you take this line and spool it straight from the package, the last color on, that is, the one you tie your leader line to, is usually white. We have found that this color is too bright and spooks some of the fish, especially the bigger ones. The next color in line is light blue—not much better.

What we do is reverse the lead core, stripping all the line from the package first, then spooling it onto the reels. This has the effect of making black the lead-core color attached to the leader, usually with dark brown as the next color in line. These darker colors do not seem to spook as many fish. There are, of course, always arguments about what color fish actually see when a line is in the water, but our success with this "line reversal" speaks for itself.

Rey C. Wojdat
Roscoe, NY

Fish Attractant for Lubrication

I know that to strengthen a knot and to help avoid any abrasions in the line, we're supposed to use our own saliva. However, what can be more foreign to the fish world than a by-product of man? Why not try some fish attractant to moisten the knot. It's more oily than your saliva, so it'll help reduce friction; it will allow you to avoid abrasions in your line and it's more common to a fish's world. It may even attract a strike from a fish that was scared off by your buddy's saliva-moistened knot.

Matt E. Farrow
Albion, NY

A fisherman just has a lot of stuff. Whether he needs it all or not is beside the point, and a different story altogether: When you have a lot of stuff, you need plenty of ideas on how to store it economically and efficiently so that a) you can find it when you need it and b) once you find it, it's in good and usable condition.

Many of the tips and ideas here are absolutely ingenious, and they will all certainly make your time on the water more organized and enjoyable.

Inexpensive Rod Case

Last spring I was scheduled to go to Canada as part of a high school graduation trip. Being on a high-schooler's budget, I decided to use my time in wood shop class to build a box to protect my rods for the trip, rather than purchase a case for more than I could afford.

I started out by using ½-inch-thick willow. The box is 42 inches long, 4 inches deep and 6 inches wide. Inside, I glued corrugated foam similar to that used in gun cases. The foam is 1½ inches thick, for a combined thickness of 3 inches. The foam holds and protects the rods nicely.

With wood, hinges and latch, the box cost me a total of $12.

Jeremy McAuliff
Kewadin, MI

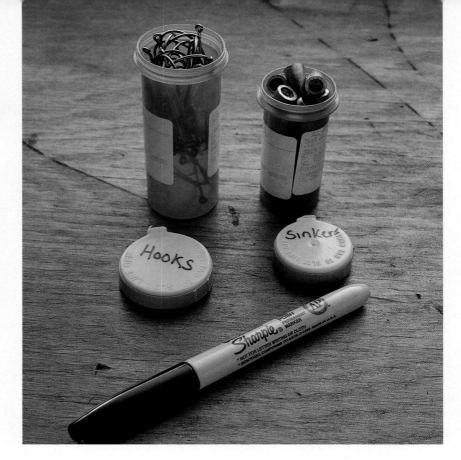

Small Storage

For a good waterproof container to store weights, matches, etc., simply use a prescription pill bottle with the childproof top. Use a waterproof marker to label the contents.

Jim Wilson
Alvarado, TX

Wader Maintenance

When you hang your waders up in a basement or a garage, they will start to deteriorate due to exposure to such substances as gas from furnaces, sunlight or just the air and its contaminants. To avoid this, store the waders in a black plastic garbage bag. Seal the bag tightly. I have done this for years, and my waders are still in great shape.

Steve vonBrandt
Wilmington, DE

Bottom-Rig File System

I have a small, open tackle box just for stowing single- and double-hook bottom rigs. I save empty wide-mouth vitamin and medicine vials and bottles.

The rigs, which are always a problem to restow in the plastic bags they came in, can easily be rolled up and inserted in the bottles. I place a small label on the outside, designating either a single- or double-hook rig. The tops also show either "1" or "2" to simplify identification. They stand up neatly in the small tackle box and are readily available without having to untangle them.

Leslie J. Richardson
San Benito, TX

Tighten Tackle Box Dividers

If you find that movable tackle box dividers keep loosening their hold, secure them with silicone. You'll be relieved to see how that keeps them in place.

Richard Labone
Monroe, NJ

Tackle Box Cleaning Tip

Clean the debris out of your tackle box without emptying it. Use a vacuum cleaner with the attachment of your choice with a fine mesh screen taped over the intake port. The screen will lift the debris without lifting the lures, sinkers, etc., leaving the box clean. Smaller items may be lifted to the surface of the screen. They may be easily removed by shutting off the vacuum. They will be cleaned in the process.

Wayne Zarbok
Canyon Lake, CA

Stow Crawler Harnesses and Leaders

I've come up with a neat, simple-to-see-your-selection and easy-to-use method of storing nightcrawler harnesses and leaders. It is also simple and inexpensive to make and will last a long time.

Cut foam-plastic insulation (I prefer ¾-inch) used in house construction to any desired size. Stick the hook in an edge of the board and wrap the line snugly around the board while being sure to only slightly space each wrap to conserve space yet make removing easy. Press a paneling nail, because it is coated to prevent rusting, through the snap or eye of the rig partially through the board to fasten. Store unused nails in the end of the board for future use. I write the length of the leader on the foam plastic.

Storing these boards on your boat can be accomplished in a special way. My wife created homemade vinyl pouches with snaps to hold them in place. She added a small pocket across the front for bottom bouncers or broken pieces of crawler harnesses to be saved and re-used. She left several inches above the snaps to act as a flap and keep the weather out. While she was at it, she made several more for the back of the boat seats for additional storage.

Mike Giamportone
Marysville, MI

Magnetize Your Tackle Box

Glue magnets to your tackle box for holding your needle-nose pliers, hook disgorger or other tools to keep them handy.

Dennis Malkin
Gates Mills, OH

Money-Saving Tackle Bag

I use a heavy-duty flat-bottom tote bag instead of those expensive angler tackle bags that range from $60 to $80. I spent $19 on one and $29 on another at the luggage department of Kmart. They have two large compartments on each end, a side zipper compartment, hold about 8 to 13 plastic trays and feature two side compartments with zippers. They come with a wide carrying strap. Mine weighs about 40 pounds and holds up very well. They last about 2 years depending on how rough you are with them. The cloth-canvas bags will last 4 to 5 years, whereas the ones with plastic don't last long. These bags are great camouflage as well, because they don't look like tackle bags when unattended. The real bags stick out like sore thumbs and attract thieves.

William Schooner
Poultney, VT

Stores Film, Then Tackle

Save your empty film containers. They are excellent for sinkers, hooks and all those small items that end up in the bottom of your tackle box.

Jeff Roye
Three Bridges, NY

Rod-Guide Protection

To protect the guides of your fishing rod when it is in a storage container, get the foam-plastic wraps that are designed for water pipes, and put that around the rods. The wraps come in different diameters, are very light and inexpensive and protect the rods very well.

John F. Toews
Omaha, NE

Tackle Storage in Tight Quarters

If you don't have room for a large tackle box in your boat, or you don't want to lug a tackle box while walking the shorelines, pick out what you need and carry it in a fishing vest.

The pockets are large enough to carry all of the spinnerbaits you need, but who wants to stick their hands into a big wad of lures and then try to untangle the mess or pull hooks out of their fingers?

To remedy this problem, I adapted a Plano 3450 Storage Box just for spinnerbaits. By carefully using an Exacto Knife or flat razor blade, you can cut the dividers approximately ⅝ to ¾ inch from the top of the compartment at a 60-degree angle down to the backside of the storage box. Then make a cut down the backside of the divider, parallel to the storage box's outside wall. The resulting cut of this flexible, yet sturdy plastic will present a groove so that you can lay your spinnerbaits down flat, with the bend of the wire being accommodated by your handiwork.

Robert A. O'Bleness
Muskogee, OK

Babying Pork Rind

I put my pork trailers in baby food jars. The lids have heavy plastic threads and do not stick. The only disadvantage is that the jars are made of glass, so handle with care.

Scott Torbeck
St. Peter, IL

Waterproof Map Holder

A great place to put a fishing map is in a modified tube from giftwrap. Put duct tape on the outside. Cover one end with duct tape. Then cut a piece off of the section of the tube that is not being used. Cover up one end of this piece with tape and line the outside with tape. Use this smaller piece as a lid. You now have a waterproof fishing map container that is light and easy to haul around.

Kevin Anderson
North Salt Lake, UT

Neat Anchor-Rope Stowage

My problem had always been storing anchor line neatly. I like to use two anchors, so that's a lot of line with which to contend. I've tried broom handles to wrap it around, 5-gallon buckets to store it in and just laying it on the bow. Nothing worked well.

It was a mess, with something always getting hung up on the anchor line. My luck has changed!

I found a device called "Cord Reel" in the electrical department at Wal-Mart. It holds 150 feet of outdoor extension cord, so it was perfect for my 165 feet of ⅜-inch anchor line.

I hold the black center handle with my left hand and simply drop the anchor overboard. The yellow outside rope-holding portion spins until the anchor hits bottom. When it's time to make a move, I pull up all the anchor line by hand, then easily crank it back on the reel for neat and out-of-the-way storage. I'm ready to drop anchor easily again at the blink of an eye.

Costing only about $5, the Cord Reel provides for neat, easy and quick anchor line storage. Too bad I didn't think of this years ago; it gives me more time to fish!

Michael Pitoscia
Bound Brook, NJ

STORAGE

Storing Soft-Plastic Baits

When storing multi-colored plastic worms, lizards or frogs, lightly coat them with vegetable oil to avoid discoloration. Vegetable oil is a biodegradable product that is thinner and lighter than most oils and is virtually odorless. Coating your bait with a couple of drops will keep the plastic moist and creates a barrier to prevent colors from running.

Cameron Mitchell
Greensboro, NC

Swimmingly Good Idea

The long foam noodles used for swimming have applications for the fisherman too. I cut them in half, then cut slits to hold my jigs. I've also used them for a dipping tray and for rod holders, too.

I suspect you could even come up with some of your own uses.

Gerald Canfield
East Stroudsburg, PA

Snelled Hook Organizer

I go to the hardware store to buy the largest piece of cork they have. That's because it is a great way for me to keep my snelled hooks in order—neat and tangle-free. I simply place the hook in the cork.

Joel Siira
Erie, PA

Soft-Plastics Sorter

I keep my soft-plastic baits rolled up in a small plastic bag sorted by color to be able to quickly see which one I want to use. This not only makes them last longer, it also helps when I need to clean out my tackle box after I've "accidentally" dropped my box in the lake. Keeping your plastics this way also eliminates that fused-together messy gook in the bottom of your tackle box.

Matt Farrow
Albion, NY

Homemade Rod Case

Rod cases can be made from 4-inch PVC pipe with caps. One cap is glued to the pipe; the other is loose with a case latch attached to it. Case latches can be purchased at a hardware store. Before gluing the end to the pipe, glue a piece of foam rubber to the inside of each cap to provide additional protection for your rods in the event the case is bumped.

Mel D. Friesen
Goshen, IN

Space-Saving Rod and Reel Storage

If your garage is cluttered or perhaps houses a workshop where sawdust flies, you'll need to find another spot to store your rods and reels. I found it convenient to utilize the wall of stairwells for hanging rods and reels. You get easy access from any level or height. Also, the tackle stays warm and clean year-round.

Bill Werres
Glendale Heights, IL

Sinker Storage

Put sinkers in old Tic-Tac containers. The flip-top aids in dispensing them.

Owen Bucher
Harleysville, PA

STORAGE

Cheap Reel Dust-Protector

In the winter months I always clean and rebuild my reels. Then they are ready to be put on the rod and hung on the wall. But dust can be a cumulative problem, and reel covers can be very expensive. So, here's what I do to solve both the dust and expense problems:

I take a zip-top storage bag and cut a hole in a bottom corner. Then I slide the bag over the reel, starting from the butt of the rod and leading with the open top of the bag. The zippered bag will close over the line and keep dust and foreign bodies off the reel.

Dennis Onner
Grand Isle, NE

Recycle Pork Rind Jars

Don't throw away empty jars from pork rind. They work great for soaking your plastics in your favorite fish scents.

Rex Ballard
Benzonia, MI

Easy Access for Fly Tying

For easy access to your buck tails when tying various streamers or jigs, just pile them in a heavy-set cup or mug on the back of your fly-tying desk. You can also store pheasant and squirrel tails this way.

Alan Vormelker
Cleveland, OH

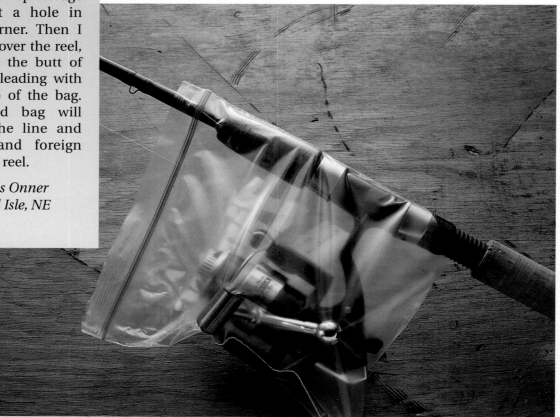

Causing a Stir

Don't throw away the paint-stir sticks—the kind with the holes in them—you get from the paint store. I make them into snelled spinner rig holders.

First, I cut off the handle. I insert the first hook on the leader into a hole, then loosely wrap the leader around the stick. With a plastic twist-tie, I secure the leader to the stick through any two holes that are convenient.

Cam Powers
Nashua, IA

Hook and Lure Hanger

During a trip to the emergency room after a Dare Devle, which I had placed on my boat seat, snagged on my anchor line and caught me as the rope slid through my hand, I conceived a better lure storage plan.

When I got back home, I cut a 1- x 1- x 12-inch piece of foam plastic and glued it to the inside of my boat by using two-part, five-minute epoxy. It's been holding for years, keeping lures and hooks off my seat and allowing for quicker tackle changes.

John M. Dugan
Monroe, CT

Pump Bottle for Fish Attractants

I like to use anise oil as an attractant, but the bottle it comes in doesn't allow me to apply it very well. In a kitchenware store I found a pump bottle for applying cooking oil. I fill the bottle half full with anise oil, then pump the top. The pressurized anise oil comes out in a fine mist.

Sean Kirwan
Canby, OR

Safe Rod and Reel Storage in Transit

After towing my boat with rods and reels rigged and locked in the rod locker, I was tired of traveling down bumpy roads, reaching my destination and finding rods, reels, lines and lures tangled.

I took some 2-inch-diameter PVC pipe and slid the rod, rigged with line and lure, tip first, into the pipe, just as far as the reel. No more tangles. It's simple, but it works.

Wayne Adams
Sanford, ME

Unique Tackle Organization

Plastic movie rental boxes can be extremely useful in organizing tackle. See if rental stores have any discards.

John Schultz
Pleasant Prairie, WI

Blanket Coverage

The next time your family buys a new blanket that comes in a clear, zippered plastic bag, save the bag. You can store rain gear and other items you want to keep dry in it. Because the bags are clear, you can easily see what you have stored. The zippered closures aid in keeping everything dry, and the bags are large enough to store several items.

Steve Helscher
Columbus Junction, IA

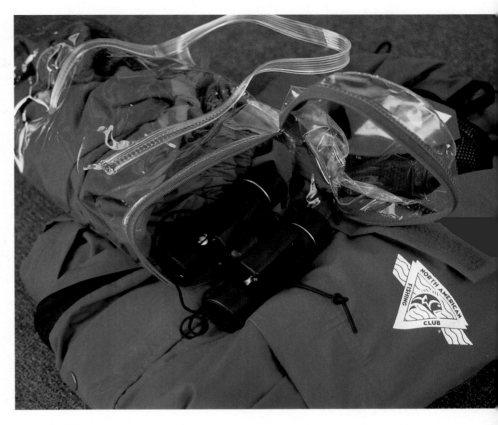

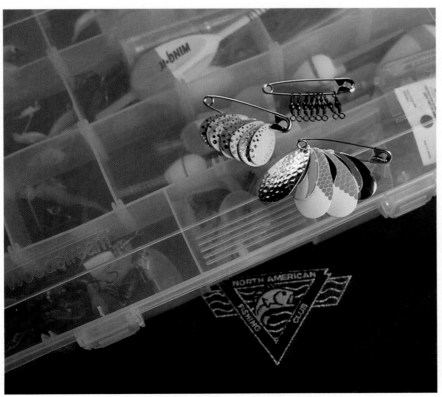

Organizing Swivels and Spinner Blades

Keep your spare spinner blades and swivels safely and neatly organized by storing them on safety pins.

Leslie J. Richardson
San Benito, TX

You don't have to have a boat to catch fish. In fact, you can often fish just as effectively from shore, or with a pair of waders on, or sitting atop a bucket on the ice. And don't let those ideas fool you … you can catch a lot of fish (some very good ones we might add) this way. How? By following the advice of people who know … learning from their strategies and ideas and then putting it all to use where you fish.

Don't feel handicapped at fishing if you don't have a boat. There are plenty of tricks-of-the-trade to help you catch fish when your feet are on shore, river-bottom, lakebottom or what we from the North like to call "the great equalizer" known as ice.

Ice-Fishing Locator Rig

When you move to a new area to ice fish, use an attractor rig to see if there are any active fish. Remove the hook from a small silver spoon. Attach a 2-inch dropper to the rear of the spoon and tie on a small ice fly or jig. Bait the fly or jig with larva. Jiggle the spoon and use a slow lift-and-drop action. The spoon's action and flash will attract fish to the fly or jig. This rig is excellent for panfish. Use a minnow on the fly or jig for walleye or sauger.

Dick Craig
Eden Prairie, MN

Dress Right for Stream Fishing

Clothing is important when fishing shallow, clearwater streams. A white T-shirt will spook every fish that sees it looming above them. A blue shirt will blend with the sky; green in wooded areas will help.

Graham McDonald
29 Palms, CA

Shore-Fish Alert

For open-bail shore fishing, I stretch the line around an aluminum can and when the fish runs, it tips the can over and no tension is felt by the fish. Not only can you see the strike, you hear it as well.

William Schooner
Poultney, VT

Environmental Wading Aid

While wading I will carry along an old broom handle with a small nail bent over in the end so that I can pick up things, like aluminum cans, that are on the bottom, polluting our fishing waters. I also occasionally pick up fishing lures with my homemade tool.

Rick C. Ruehle
Cecil, WI

Shore-Fishing Strike Indicator

When I have two rods rigged with live bait set up in different spots, and I'm free-spooling, I tie a small piece of high-visibility ribbon to the line just off the end of the rod. When a fish hits the bait, the ribbon will start to move out. When I reel in the fish, the ribbon only goes as far as the first eye. Tie it on just firmly enough to hold on the line without sliding.

Karl Ulmer
Hawley, PA

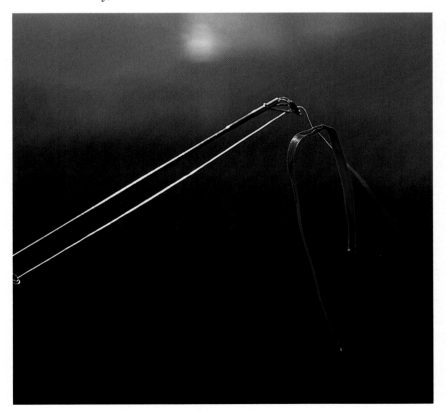

"Y" Didn't I Think of That?

A simple idea, well known by many, but perhaps not by you, is for steadying rods while shore fishing to allow for hands-free angling.

Simply find a stick with a Y-shaped fork. Stick it in the ground, and balance your fishing rod in the "V." This is of particular value if you are fishing more than one rod.

Ilinda Becker
Evansville, IN

SHORE FISHING, WADING & ICE FISHING

Wear Your Tackle

When shore fishing, carry some of your favorite baits in one or two worm boxes on a belt instead of in tackle boxes. This will leave you a free hand for getting around shrubs, and you don't have to worry about your tackle box sliding off a rock into the water.

Gerald A. Cramer
Palatine Bridge, NY

Hard-Water Fish Finder

If you have a portable fish locator, don't put it away during ice-fishing season. I've found that when you run it over wet or slushy ice, it works as well as when it's in the water. As long as the transducer (which is on the bottom) is wet and in contact with clear or moderately clear ice, it will read through the ice. What's nice about the Bottom Line Fishing Buddy is that with the shaft fully extended, you can walk around with it on the ice, scanning the bottom as you go, like a metal detector, without hunching over. If the ice isn't wet or slushy, a bottle of Epsom salts and water carried around and squirted on the ice melts it, as long as the temperature is above 15°F or so. If it's colder, some environmentally safe antifreeze and water works as well.

Once you have a few holes in the ice, you can walk around and check them with the locator. Tilting the locator will help give you an idea of whether there are any fish hanging around just outside your hole.

Frank Russo
Pompton Lakes, NJ

Do-It-Yourself Tip-Up

How to make an inexpensive tip-up. Materials needed:

- Fishing Yo-Yo's (can be ordered from Cabela's or Bass Pro)
- Two 1¼-inch x ¾-inch x 14-inch pieces pine or hardwood
- One ¼-inch (20 treads per inch) x 2½-inch eyebolt
- One eye screw, which has an opening to accommodate the line

1. Attach the Fishing Yo-Yo to one end and run the line down through the eyes. Reattach the swivel.
2. Join the two 1¼ x ¾s after drilling a ¼-inch hole with a ¼-inch 20 tpi x 2½-inch eyebolt.
3. Secure a screw eye on the opposite end of the Fishing Yo-Yo.

Bob Hawkins
Valley, NE

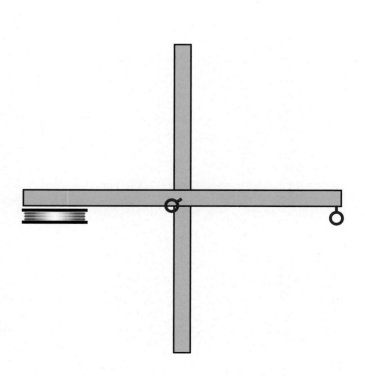

Sweeten Your Ice-Fishing Hole

When ice fishing, I occasionally sprinkle cornmeal in the hole. The meal slowly sinks, little by little, and attracts fish of all sizes, though mainly small ones—which attract the big ones. Check local regulations to make sure this is legal where you fish.

Jeff Grzeskowiak
Marysville, OH

Solution in a Bucket

My teenage son and I fish the banks of the Great Miami River for a diverse selection of species, including walleye, saugeye, largemouth and smallmouth bass, white bass, channel and flathead cats, sheepshead, gar, carp and bluegill. We had a bit of a problem to overcome. The city of Hamilton built and lined the banks with large boulders and riprap, then covered most of it up with excess concrete from other projects. This makes for some excellent places to stand when casting plugs, jigs or minnows, but there are no places to set up a rod holder because of the concrete. Laying the rods down is not an option because we usually are trying for 20-plus-pound cats with tightline drop rigs while casting the ripples for other game with light tackle.

The solution was a simple addition to the 5-gallon bucket in which we usually carry bait and lunch. We retrieve some of the fist-size and larger loose river rocks to fill the bucket. We stand 24-inch-long sections of PVC pipe, which serve as rodholders, inside the bucket. The pipes can be spaced to your liking with the rocks (vertically or splayed in an angled arc), and the bucket is very stable when filled and set on a reasonably flat section of the rough concrete. Using cutbait, minnows, liver, worms, etc., we are able to set a rig for big catfish without damage or loss, while we have hands free to cast for walleye and bass. The fun really gets going when we get four fish on simultaneously! When the day is over, dump out the rocks and use the bucket to take your gear or fish home.

Dennis J. Malone
Hamilton, OH

Walk Softly

Many anglers who fish from the bank wear dark or even camouflage clothing and are careful to duck down, but they often forget the element of sound. You also have to walk softly, even more softly than you might imagine when on soft, boggy ground. Fish can feel the vibrations of your footsteps, and even if they don't spook, they become cautious and difficult to catch.

Steve vonBrandt
Wilmington, DE

Keep Your Transducer on Ice

When ice fishing, I drill a hole a few inches deep next to and connecting to the hole I am fishing. I can then put the transducer of my fish finder on the ice in this new partial hole. It will allow for an accurate reading, yet be out of the way when I am bringing a fish through the main hole.

Greg Stetz
Pelican Rapids, MN

Rod Insurance

When my wife and I arrived at a favorite striped bass fishing spot on the Sacramento delta, we cast out our lines, then started to set up camp. We were using 13-foot surf rods and 20-pound-test line on a loosely set drag, because you never know when a 40-pound striper might come along.

When I turned around to check my rod, it was gone. We saw it in the water, slowly moving with the outgoing tide. I ran down the shoreline to grab my rod, but I couldn't reach it. Not wanting to lose my fishing rod, I jumped in, grabbed my fishing rod in about 10 to 15 feet of water and set the hook. I reeled while trying to stay afloat, all the while battling my fish.

Now when I set my fishing rod in its holder on the shore, I tie a small rope to my fishing rod and to the bumper of my truck, just in case that 40-pound striper shows up.

Michael Dokken
San Jose, CA

Shake, Rattle and Roll-Cast

The roll-cast is useful in fly-fishing when the backcast is obstructed. To make a perfect roll-cast, shake the line out on the water, then lift the fly rod in the 2 o'clock position, holding the arm high until the belly of the line sags back past your body. When the line sag passes you, flip the fly rod down fast while extending your arm outward, ending with the rod tip pointed at your target.

Ben Hankes
Beaver Dam, WI

Aluminum Can Fish Alarm

I have used this can alarm for many years and have landed countless fish with it. One time, after falling asleep while catfishing at night, the can alarm was set off at 3 a.m. and rattled down the bank to the lake as I jumped up and set the hook on a 3-pound channel catfish. Here's how you can make this simple strike indicator.

Put several, but not too many, small pebbles into an empty soda or beer can to give it some weight. Rattle the can to check how noisy it will be. Next, stand the can alongside your rod near the reel. Bend the flip-top tab upward until its nearly straight up. Pull about 2 feet of your line from the spool, bring the line around the tab of the can and take up the slack by pulling the can away from the rod until the can is in position to fall over at the slightest nibble from a fish.

As the fish takes the bait, the can should be knocked over, releasing the line and making quite a racket as the pebbles inside the can rattle.

Thomas Hartinger
Tucson, AZ

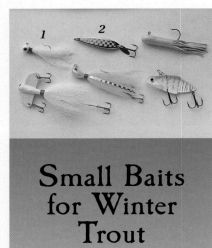

Small Baits for Winter Trout

When ice fishing, use small baits. Winter fish are not particularly hungry because of a slower metabolism. They will pass up large entrees, in favor of some tasty appetizers.

David Harden
Littleton, CO

Summer "Ice Fishing"

I do a lot of fishing on trout streams in northern Wisconsin's national forests. These streams are kept very natural and can be very overgrown in places, with trees and bushes hanging over the stream. This makes it impossible to use a fly rod and difficult to use a spinning rod. To alleviate this problem, I have found that my ice-fishing jigging pole, a 2½-foot Ugly Stik with an ultralight spinning wheel, works perfectly for these tight situations. It also makes landing larger trout more challenging.

Gary Christopher
Muskego, WI

Cast from a Distance

When approaching a shoreline, cast your bait or artificial lure in the water before you actually walk up to the water. Many times you can catch a fish or two in the shallows by walking all the way to the bank. This also helps when the sun is at your back because your shadow will spook fish. This approach has helped me enjoy my fishing over the years, especially with larger fish that happen to be cruising the shallows.

T. Lewis
Bakersfield, CA

Flies through the Ice

If you like to use flies in open water, don't be surprised to learn they can catch fish through the ice also. I have only experimented on perch and bluegills, but other flies may work on other species. In any case, flies may be used on conventional ice fishing jigging outfits.

The flies I have tied and tried that have caught fish are the Crazy Charlie and Clouser Minnow. These patterns have the barbell (or hourglass) or bead-chain eyes, dressed with marabou or hair for extra "life" in the water. The barbells and beads contribute weight, which allows the flies to be fished as a small jig. Silver, brown and pearl bodies with added sparkle from "Krystal Flash" or "Flashabou" mixed in the marabou or hair wing seem to work well. Flies imitating the colors of the minnows in the bucket (and in the lake) seem to get the most strikes. For some odd reason, the perch in the lake I fish really enjoy bonefish-type fly patterns, in 4-8 hook sizes, through the ice. I use the flies without added bait. However, adding a spike, grub or other bait to a fly, though it goes against the grain of a fly fishing purist, is worthy of experimentation.

Matt Gregory
Palatine, IL

Add Flash to Your Ice Fishing

When ice fishing, tie a piece of tinsel just above the lure. It suspends and has a wave-like flash that will attract more fish.

Rey C. Wojdat
Roscoe, NY

Anatomy of a Gravel Pit

One of my favorite sports is ice fishing for trout, and one of my favorite places to do it is in a gravel pit. Here's what I've learned about locating fish.

Trout hang around walls, mounds and river inlets. Some of their favorite spots include the walls of the gravel pit, where the surrounding water is 6 to 8 feet deep, but the center of the pit is 30 feet deep. I fish the wall in 16 feet of water.

Another productive spot is a point coming off a wall. Fish seem to follow the bay and concentrate on the point.

A mound along the wall is another favorite spot. Although the mound is small, 3 to 4 feet, it holds fish.

I also like river inlets. They bring in food and oxygen, but caution needs to be exercised, because the ice may be dangerously thin here.

You may be able to apply this analysis to your favorite ice fishing trout water.

David Harden
Littleton, CO

Combo Net and Walking/ Wading Staff

I fish an upland reservoir, because it is close to home, but its riprap shoreline makes tough going for a 73-year-old like me. I use a landing net with a 4-foot handle for a walking stick to help get me around the reservoir.

To keep from wearing out the net on the rocks I take a piece of ⅝-inch garden hose about 12 inches long and slit it endwise and fasten it to the top of the net by using copper wire.

When fishing for smallmouth bass in creeks and rivers, I use a smaller, shorter-handled net for the same purpose. This net has a clip on the handle to fasten to my suspenders while I'm fishing.

Clyde King
Tiffin, OH

Stealth in the Water

Catching stream fish requires a subtle approach.

Fishermen who wear camouflage or muted colors and try to blend in with their background can get closer to fish in clear water without spooking them than anglers who don't. Getting closer lets a fisherman achieve shorter, more accurate casts, which are less likely to alarm fish.

Fish can detect the vibrations and grating sounds of wading anglers from farther away than you can cast. To overcome the fish's natural tendency to spook, stand still for long periods when casting and move only a few steps at a time. Fish lose their fear within a few minutes if the sounds are not repeated.

Don't wade in the water before you fish in it. Big fish often lie in the shallows, where they are quickly disturbed by wading fishermen. You can avoid spooking them by making a few surreptitious casts before covering the water you plan to enter.

Ben Hankes
Beaver Dam, WI

Weighty Words from a Heavy Mouth

I fly fish for steelhead in northeast Ohio in many of the colder months. That means I am wearing neoprene gloves to cut the wind chill. Weighting your fly is extremely important, but it can be very time consuming, in fact, next to impossible, with gloves on.

I've long been a fan of Loon Outdoors non-toxic Deep Soft Weight, but it has a tendency to get rock hard in cold weather. Now I simply keep a pliable hunk in my mouth, so I am ready to bite off the desired amount to easily weight my fly for an optimum drift.

Alan Vormelker
Cleveland, OH

Make Steel Rod Holders Hold

The steel rod fishing-rod holders sometimes won't push into hard ground or gravel. To remedy this, take the rod holder, and bend the bottom 2 inches at opposite 90-degree angles. Place the rod holder in an empty coffee can and fill the can with cement.

The holder can be used on most surfaces, because of the weight of the cement and the flat bottom of the can.

Thomas Turpie
Pittsburgh, PA

Wading Belt Rod Holder

I do a lot of wading for walleyes in the spring and fall, and I created a device that really comes in handy, because it allows me to put the butt of my fishing rod in it, freeing up both hands to unhook a fish, rebait or change lures. This belt is fairly easy to make and can be conveniently pushed out of the way when you are wearing it.

To make one, simply fasten a small piece of plexiglass and a 10-inch length of 1¼-inch-diameter PVC pipe to a wide web belt.

Wear this belt for hands-free opportunities.

G. C. Lazier
Cortland, OH

An old sage once said, "You have two great days as a boat owner: the day you get it, and the day you get rid of it." Which implies that everything in between is hard work. Which it is. But it's necessary work. Maintaining a boat, and learning its ins and outs, takes a lot of time, knowledge and insight. That's the kind of knowledge that members and pros share here.

And if you've always thought of getting a nice rig but the budget wasn't quite right, you'll want to take a look at the special bonus section here, "Build Your Own Customized Riverboat" (page 116). Even if you're not a river fisherman, the ideas here will transfer well to most any basic boat you want to "fix up" and make a little more comfortable and functional.

Don't Let Trailer Wires Be a Drag

To keep my trailer light pigtail wiring from dragging on the ground, I hang it from my rear bumper with an old shower hook. I simply use an existing hole and run the hook between the wires and clip. In that way you can remove the wiring easily to hook up your trailer.

Rick C. Ruehle
Cecil, WI

Extension-Cord Storage

On long fishing trips where you need an extension cord to run a battery charger or lights, carrying a wad of cords can be a tangle. A modified 5-gallon bucket makes an excellent organizer for your cords.

Drill or cut a 2-inch hole at the base of the bucket and, leaving a couple of feet of slack, insert the male end of the cord through the hole. Then coil the rest of your cords into the bucket as you would lay a hand coil. The bucket will hold 300 to 400 feet of cord.

James Jared
Oxford, NY

On-the-Spot Scent Holder

I was often irritated with the sticky, messy condition of my bait attractant bottles while fishing. A couple of years ago I came up with this solution:

Pick up an inexpensive car ashtray, the type that is tin, attached to a beanbag bottom, designed to sit on the dashboard of a car. They do a great job of staying put on the floor of a boat as well!

At the beginning of the fishing trip, pour attractant into the ashtray once, then throughout the day all that is needed to scent your bait is a quick dip in the ashtray, keeping your hands free from becoming covered in the liquid and making application much quicker and easier. I keep one ashtray in the front of my boat and another in the rear—no more mess and no more passing the bottle to your bud in the back! And, if you fish often enough, you don't even have to add attractant every trip; the ashtray stays put and holds the liquid for days.

Worth Canoy
High Point, NC

Paint Your Downrigger Balls

If you are a Great Lakes troller, try this tip. It helped me win $82,000 Canadian dollars!

Paint the cannonballs of your downriggers, first with a couple of white undercoats, then with a glow-in-the-dark color.

I believe this modification to my downrigger weights helped attract the 40.05-pound chinook salmon I caught in Lake Ontario during the Toronto Star Salmon Derby in August, 1998.

William J. Beacham
Dundas, Ontario

Rope Ladder for Boating Safety

Did you ever try to get back into a boat if you've fallen overboard? It is nearly impossible if you are by yourself. I have mounted a rope ladder to the rear pedestal of my boat. It can be reached from either side. If I make a grab, I can reach the ladder. When it is not in use, I roll it up in a small package, which fits in storage.

James Kleinman
West Portsmouth, OH

≋ ADVICE FROM THE PROS ≋

Sock It to 'Em

When drift fishing with live bait, use a drift sock in high winds. It deploys like a parachute and fills with water to provide enough drag to slow the speed of your boat and your bait.

Ted Takasaki
NAFC Walleye Advisory Council

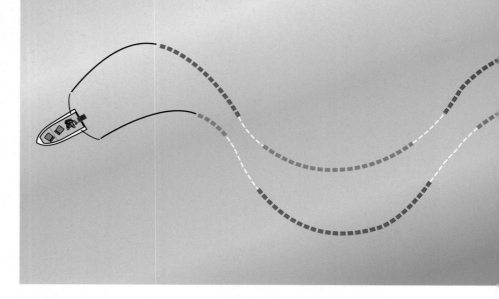

Yet Another Use for WD-40

On a trip to Barkley Lake we left the portable depth finder next to the battery while the battery was being charged. The next morning the lens was clouded, and the casing and lens had white dots all over them. No matter what cleaning agents we used, nothing would clean my depth finder. I contacted the manufacturer, who gave me a price of $97 plus shipping to change the lens. Upon returning home I continued trying to clean the lens and casing. Finally I tried WD-40. I sprayed it on, and instantly it cleared the lens and made the casing look new. Now every couple of months, I just spray the depth finder to keep it looking nice.

Roger Dietrich
Cincinnati, OH

Trolling Different Depths

When you are trolling, your fish finder may indicate fish at levels varying by as much as 10 to 20 feet. Changing weights is time consuming. I have had success in increasing my catch by zigzagging the boat to the left and then to the right for about 10-second intervals. The bait drops as the tension on the line is released each time you turn the boat and then rises as you straighten out for the 10-second interval. This procedure also gives an erratic motion to your bait and increases your chance of a strike.

Pete Slempa
Chehalis, WA

ADVICE FROM THE PROS

Boat Control for Jig Fishing

When jigging in rivers, a boat-control technique known as "slipping" or "chasing your line" can help you feel every bite and set the hook quickly. Point your bow into the current, let your jig fall to the bottom, engage your reel and take out the slack. Each time you drop your rod tip, you should see a slight bow in your line. Use short bursts with an electric bow-mounted trolling motor to stay directly over your jig as you move downstream with the current.

Ted Takasaki
NAFC Walleye Advisory Council

Stake Your Boat

When you need to secure your beached boat, or when loading or unloading by yourself, a pet stake can help. These pet stakes are corkscrew-shaped and designed to be screwed into the ground to leash or rope your dog. Screw the pet stake into the ground and tie off the boat, allowing the solitary angler to back the trailer into the water or to relax on the shore.

Jacob Sheehan
Eastford, CT

Salmon Trolling Secret

When trolling for salmon, finding the bait is the key. Pay attention to our electronics when crossing over large schools of bait. Salmon will attack the bait schools with slashing jaws and tails, crippling as many as they can. The larger fish cruise beneath the schools of bait and pick off the slowly sinking cripples. When you see a large school of bait on the depth finder, kick your boat into neutral and let your lines sink beneath the school. Try 20- to 30-second pauses for starters, increasing up to a minute if necessary. You can trigger strikes from the larger fish when your bait or lure starts slowing down and sinking like a cripple. The big fish can also be triggered into striking after you engage your engine, bringing your baits or lures back up the water column.

William L. McCabe
Napa, CA

Sticky Solution

When putting on boat numbers, decals or stripes, clean the surface, then spray a fine mist of Windex on the area. Position the item, and slide it to the exact spot. Smooth out any air pockets and let dry. It will now stay as placed.

Tony Bennett
Muskego, WI

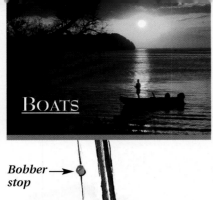

BOATS

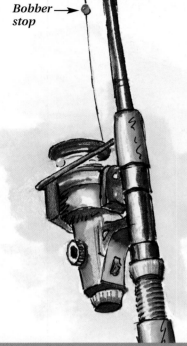

Bobber stop →

Fishing Tool Organizer

It's a rule of thumb: No matter where you are when you boat a fish, your tools are always somewhere else or just out of reach. To solve the problem, try this easy solution: Take 2-inch PVC pipe and cut it into five pieces each 8 inches long. Place each of the pieces on an end around the base of the shaft of your seat or pedestal. Mark where each pipe touches the ones next to it at the bottom. Then drill holes and insert small nuts and screws. Once secured, the five-tool holder is easy to set up and take down, simply by lifting out the seat. Never be out of reach of your tools or that special lure again. And while you have the do-it-yourself spirit, screw a couple of cup hangers under your seat or pedestal—perfect storage spots for hanging line clippers and other small tools.

Bruce A. Kitowski
St. Joseph, MN

Cross Your Trailer Chains

When I hitch up a trailer, I will always cross the safety chains in an "X." This creates a cradle, just in case the trailer does come off the hitch ball. I also put a little grease on the hitch ball to keep it moving freely while I am making turns.

Rick C. Ruehle
Cecil, WI

Consistent Trolling Depth

The amount of line that you have out when trolling will change the depth to which your lure will travel. Put slip-bobber stops on the fishing line of your trolling rigs. They are fast and easy to adjust and will not interfere with the playing of fish. Best of all, you can get back to the depth that you were at quickly and accurately and catch more fish.

Joe Adams
Tulia, TX

ADVICE FROM THE PROS

Keep Grass off Your Lure

Shad fishermen on the Delaware River anchor and fish darts and flutter spoons in the current. To ward off grass and other debris from fouling their hooks, knowledgeable anglers half-hitch a rubber band onto their line a foot or two above their lure. It catches and deflects any debris flowing from upriver.

Glenn Sapir
Putnam Valley, NY

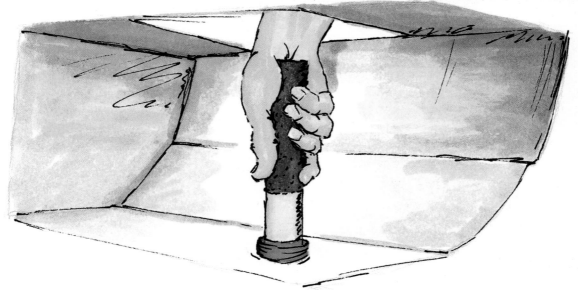

Unscrewing Stubborn Live Well Plugs

I solved the problem of removing the drain plugs from the live wells in my boat. The drain plugs are hard plastic with an overflow slot at the top and threaded end at the bottom, and they screw securely into the drain of the live well. Gripping the smooth plastic plugs when they were wet was difficult, but I needed to do it to remove the plugs to drain the live well. I tried roughing the plastic surface, but that was not sufficient.

Then I hit upon a great solution. I glued a piece of coarse-grit abrasive cloth completely around the upper portion of each drain plug. I used a glue gun glue that I felt confident would not soften with continuous immersion in water when the live well was full.

Since I've incorporated this modification, the drain plugs come out easily, without my having to use locking pliers or other tools.

Joe Zwack
St. Paul, MN

≈ ADVICE FROM ≈
THE PROS

Advice for the Launch Ramp

When backing your boat down the ramp, and your vehicle begins to slide, slip the vehicle into neutral and the sliding will stop. When ready to pull out, back up just a little to make sure the boat is released completely from the trailer and then exit the ramp slowly, in case your partner forgot to untie the tiedowns and winch rope.

Jimmy Houston
Cookson, OK

A Clean Live Well

Here is a tip to keep your live well clean and fresh. At the end of the fishing day, drain the live well and refill it with fresh water until it is three-quarters full. Then add a box of baking soda. During the drive home, the mixture will slosh around, cleaning the walls of the live well. When you get home, drain the live well and rinse it thoroughly with fresh water.

Jacob Sheehan
Eastford, CT

Trailering Aid

Most anglers learn when backing a trailer to use their car mirrors. Sometimes using mirrors is wise, but there are times when it's not. Having been a heavy-equipment operator for the Air Force, I know that backing a trailer this way is not only impractical, but unsafe.

I have a small 8- x 10-foot trailer that I use for my jon boat. It's not wide enough to see in my mirrors, and when the boat is off, the trailer disappears in the mirrors. I remedied this by placing my fishing bag on the middle of the back of my little trailer. Now by turning around in my seat I can see my fishing bag and be safe by knowing that if I keep the bag in the middle of my rear window, my trailer is going where I want it to go, and I can clearly see throughout my whole field of vision. By backing my trailer this way, there are no surprises!

Matt Farrow
Albion, NY

Trailer Guides

You can make boat-trailer guides using PVC pipe. To flatten the end of a pipe so you can attach it to another object with screws and washers, boil water in a pot and place the end of the pipe in the water until it softens. When it is soft, you immediately put it in a vise and flatten it, leaving it in the vise until it cools. If you do not like the outcome of the pipe, place the pipe back in the water, and it will return to the original shape.

For boat guides, a short section flattened and glued on a 45° angle with a longer section attached to the other side of the 45° angle, with a cap glued on the end make nice boat guides for trailers. Measure to allow 2 inches from the side of the boat and 2 inches higher than the boat. Attach flattened end to the trailer frame.

Reflective strips (white on front, red on back of pipe) help other vehicles to see the boat and trailer when you are trailering at night. The white strips will pick up your backup lights at night when putting the trailer in the water.

Roger Dietrich
Cincinnati, OH

Slide through the Water

I don't wax my boat below the waterline. I use silicone. It makes the boat slide better through the water.

Scott Wilton
Clearwater, FL

Consistent Flat Lines

Here's a tip that worked well for me over the years as a charter-boat captain fishing for salmon in Lake Michigan:

When using surface or, what they are more aptly called, flat lines on Lake Michigan, I had to be able to return the line to the same depth as where the first fish was caught. Different amounts of line out would place the lure at different depths, so maintaining a predetermined amount of line out was important, but difficult and time consuming. So, here's what you should do.

Take your reel and turn the handle until the level wind is at its return point axis, either to the far left or far right, the side doesn't matter. Then go to the tip of the rod that you are using, and pull a length of line off of the reel until the level wind reaches the exact opposite end of the reel. Measure that length of line back to the rod tip (usually between 7 and 10 feet). Now, by counting each pass of the level wind you can measure within a few inches of where your lure will be; i.e., 8 feet of line times 10 passes equals 80 feet. In this way you can predetermine the amount of line you want out—and return to it every time.

Herman J. Kunz
Fairfield, IL

Shore Up Your Anchor

Do you have problems keeping a good hold on the bottom with your fold-up anchor? Try this:

Replace the first 5 feet of anchor rope with chain. This weighs down the top of the anchor, allowing it to lie down so it can dig into the bottom.

Bob Caldwell
Longview, WA

ADVICE FROM THE PROS

Walleye Speed Limits

Lure speed is one of the variables anglers can control when trolling for walleyes. When pulling crankbaits, stay within the range of 1½ to 3 mph. Spinner rigs should be trolled more slowly. The rule of thumb is in colder water, go slower; in warmer water, go faster. Tournament pros have found, however, that trolling fast, even in frigid water, may be the key to trigger strikes. Likewise, a snail's pace may produce on a hot day. So, don't be afraid to experiment.

Troll in subtle "S" turns. In that way, baits on the inside travel slower and baits on the outside travel faster. Pay attention to see if bites come on one side or the other.

Ted Takasaki
NAFC Walleye Advisory Council

Versatile Bucket

I store my anchor rope in a 5-gallon plastic pail, by just curling up the rope inside it. I also use the bucket on windy days in a different way. I attach the anchor rope to its handle and hang it over the bottom to slow the boat while it's drifting. I have a quick connector so I can unclip the rope from the anchor to the bucket and back. The pail works just as well as an expensive drift sock for a small boat.

Joe Tury
Warren, OH

Table Talk

The floor in my wooden boat has removable floor sections to facilitate cleaning and drying after each fishing trip. I added four folding legs to the bottom side of the smallest piece. It is used as a low table for shore lunches. Just remove it from the boat, fold down the legs, cover with a tablecloth and presto: A table for shore lunches that doubles as a vital element of the boat without cluttering a full boat.

Mel D. Friesen
Goshen, IN

Whitecaps, White Crappie

Have you ever gotten up to go bass fishing only to find the wind howling out of the east at about 25 to 30 mph, and decided not to go? Or, have you ever been on a big body of water when the wind came up and made it impossible to fish the only shoreline where you had been catching bass?

The next time this happens to you, don't stay home or pack up and leave; use the whitecaps to your advantage for white crappie!

If you are on a strange

body of water, you will have to use your graph to locate the appropriate structure for crappie in that particular area. If you are fishing a local lake or other familiar body of water, then your task will of course be much easier.

After locating your spot, toss out two marker buoys on either side of the brush pile or other structure as target lanes. Anchor your boat appropriately fore and aft.

Your standard crappie jigs that work in your particular area will do just fine. However, I suggest a good quality 6- to 6½-foot graphite rod and a quality spinning reel, spooled with braided line of 10-pound test. Once you locate the depth you want to fish, simply set your rods down on the side of the boat and pay attention to your lines. The wave action will do all the work for you. Simply pick up the pole when the line does anything at all that it hasn't been doing previously—and there will be a crappie on it. It's that simple! Turn a lousy day of bass fishing into a good day of crappie fishing! Who knows? You just might catch a bass or two also. Many times using this method, I've caught big bass on small crappie jigs. Sometimes good things come from adversity.

Steve vonBrandt
Wilmington, DE

Speed Up to Remedy Short Salmon Strikes

If you are trolling baits, such as herring or anchovies, salmon can strike at your baits, leaving a scratch or two as evidence. Salmon won't come back for a second strike on a scratched bait. Increasing your trolling speed forces the fish to be more aggressive while chasing your bait. A little more trolling speed will cure the problem.

William L. McCabe
Napa, CA

Protect Your Boat Wires

To keep the wires in your boat from getting stepped on and broken, run the wires through some automotive hoses. Take a ⅜-inch rubber gas-line hose and cut it along the entire length. Then slip it over the wires and use electrical tape to keep it closed and tight. The hoses cushion the wires and may save you some electrical problems later.

Steve vonBrandt
Wilmington, DE

Removable Boat-Floor Covers

To help cut down on the noise from the floor of any aluminum boat, cut up an old rubber bed mat from a pickup truck. I cut mine into three strips to fit neatly between the seats of my 14-foot boat. The pickup bed mat not only helps cut down the noise, but it also can easily be rolled up and hosed off for easy cleanup. Old rubber floor mats can also be used to buffer the noise from portable gas tanks and batteries.

Matt Radzialowski
Wixom, MI

≋ ADVICE FROM THE PROS ≋

Debris-Free Crankbaits

When trolling crankbaits in rivers, try pinching a small split-shot about 2 feet above the lure to intercept floating debris and prevent your bait from fouling. Watch your rod tips; when they stop vibrating, it's time to clean off your hooks.

Ted Takasaki
NAFC Walleye Advisory Council

BOATS

Chumming Around

A mixture of oatmeal, moistened with a combination of garlic powder and water, makes a great chum. The garlic powder and water mixture also makes an effective dip for live or artificial bait.

Ross Gough
Key West, FL

A Better Battery Connection

Ever have the alligator clips make crackling noises after turning the battery charger on? It's because the alligator clip is not making a good connection. It's happened to me, and I did something about it. My solution gives me a solid connection every time. It won't fall off the battery, there's no chance of getting sparks and charging is more efficient. Here's what I did:

I cut the cable about 16 inches from the alligator clips. Then I attached a two-pin male Molex connector to the end of the cable going toward the battery charger. I placed a two-pin female Molex connector on the cable going to the alligator clips. Then, the most important part: I took two 16-inch pieces of 16-gauge wire and placed them on a two-pin female Molex connector. To the other end of the two wires I attached ring lugs.

Now, when I connect the adapter cable to the battery charger, I get a solid connection.

John M. Dugan
Monroe, CT

≋ **ADVICE FROM THE PROS** ≋

Net Results

A critical moment in the fishing process comes after you've reeled your fish to the side of the boat. More fish are lost then than at any other time. As you carefully reel in line or raise your rod high to bring the fish to the surface, your partner should be visualizing that his task is to net the water around the fish, not the fish itself. When you think about trying to net the fish, you sometimes wind up hitting it with the metal hoop of the net and knocking it free.

Another mistake made boatside is letting the fish thrash on the surface. Leave enough line to keep them under the surface until the net is ready.

Ted Takasaki
NAFC Walleye Advisory Council

Pull for Efficiency

Electric motors are more efficient when pulling a boat rather than pushing it.

Jacob Sheehan
Eastford, CT

Keep Lures Handy

When going out in your boat fishing, get a 12- x 12- x 2-inch-thick foam-plastic square from a craft supply store. Attach an eye hook on opposite sides and strap it to a boat seat with a bungee cord. What you have created is a handy lure storage board.

Take the few lures you use most frequently and press the hooks into the foam. The lures will be secured and can be easily removed; they will not fall off the board.

This will save you from fumbling through your tackle box and wasting precious fishing time and prevent the noise of going through a tackle box. Your lures will be close at hand.

Lewis Krystyniak
Palos Heights, IL

Duct-Tape Anchor

My friend and I fish Colorado reservoirs from a vinyl boat with an electric motor. One time we launched without our anchor. My companion had a makeshift solution, thanks to a roll of duct tape he had brought. He fashioned a 20-foot "rope" with the tape and wrapped one end around a rock anchor. It worked perfectly, even with a fair breeze.

Marlin C. Sigaty
Colorado Springs, CO

ADVICE FROM THE PROS

"Running" in the Wind

When running into the wind and the water is white-capping, move within a safe distance from the bank. Get out of the middle of the lake and run the shorelines. Be careful of obstacles and keep a safe distance out. The water is less choppy on the shorelines. Never run perpendicular to white caps—unless you enjoy swimming and being completely soaked.

Jimmy Houston
Cookson, OK

Build Your Own Customized River Boat

There's something about fishing a river. The moving water just seems more exciting. Fish—from cats to smallmouth to walleyes to panfish and more—abound. There's always an interesting fish to target, and usually a variety of others available to mix up the bag and keep things exciting. Plus, it seems that rivers just don't get as much fishing pressure as the lakes, reservoirs and ponds and other still water that everybody seems to focus on.

There's every reason to fish rivers, but why aren't more of us doing it? We at the NAFC came up with at least one theory, and it's certainly true to some extent: Many of us just aren't outfitted with a proper boat for effective river fishing.

For instance, there's a river near NAFC Headquarters that's loaded with big small-mouths. On a good day you can catch dozens, as well as the odd cat, walleye and carp. What's more, despite slicing through the backyards of about a million anglers, the waters go virtually unfished.

Why? Rocks, which by themselves wouldn't be so bad, but many of them lie just inches beneath the surface where they eat any deep-v or bass boat that dares enter. Most anglers run those types of craft, which puts them out of the game immediately.

And we aren't unique here in our neck of the woods. Rivers across the country abound with challenges as daunting as those rocks: sandbars, wingdams, inches-shallow bays, tidal flats, muddy shoals, snags, stick-ups, assorted downed trees … fish heaven but a real boating challenge. It's no wonder rivers are underfished!

So we decided to create a great river boat. That the craft would be a jonboat was a given. A jon's shallow draft, light weight and ability to handle current made it the perfect choice. Although it's just a river-fishing outfit, when we finished the boat it had a flat, carpeted floor, rod holders, a bow-mounted trolling motor, and a baitwell

Editor's Note:

In addition to all the superb member fishing tips within this book, we wanted to add even more value for NAFC members. You're looking at the result! Maybe you'll build this river boat start to finish, or maybe you'll just take some of the ideas and adapt them to your own rig. Either way, the detailed instructions in this project will help you customize a fishing rig you can be proud of … and use to really catch more fish!

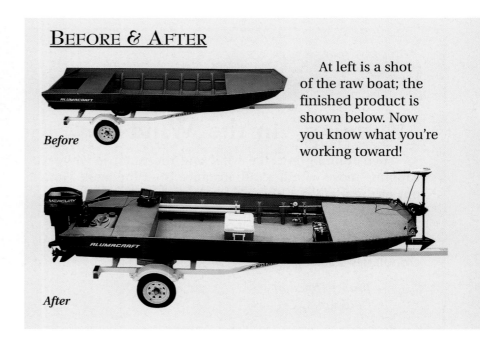

BEFORE & AFTER

Before

After

At left is a shot of the raw boat; the finished product is shown below. Now you know what you're working toward!

with an aeration system. Fairly fancy, but economical too.

We chose the Alumacraft 1542 NCS as the basic boat for a number of reasons: the folks in their Arkadelphia, Arkansas, plant know how to build a jonboat that can take the abuses that rivers dish out; the dimensions and layout fit what we were looking for; the 15-foot hull weighs just 230 pounds, and our rigging added only minimal extra weight (about 70 pounds with battery); and the boat is still easy to drag over shallow shoals and fallen trees.

The floor is 42 inches wide and nearly 8 feet long, which means there's plenty of room to fish comfortably and efficiently. Plus, the bow deck and oversize rear seat offer elevated casting platforms. The hull is rated for a 25-horsepower tiller outboard, but a 15 or 20 offers enough get-up-and-go without extra weight.

To tow it, we bought a Spartan B-14 trailer, a no-frills model with a load capacity of 1,000 pounds, more than enough to handle the boat, motor (we picked the 20-horsepower Mercury), and your gear.

Is this the perfect river boat? If not, it's close. And that's the beauty of building your own: Adjust and adapt as necessary for your particular needs!

See ya on the river.

Tools and Materials Needed

Tools

Depending on what you do to your boat, the list of tools you'll need will vary somewhat from those we used. The basic list includes: an electric and/or cordless drill (having two speeds things up); drill bits; circular saw; jigsaw; hacksaw; 2-inch hole saw; screwdrivers (a cordless drill/driver is even better); staple gun; wire stripper/crimper; tape measure; snapline; straight-edge yardstick; carpet and utility knives; coffee can filled with sand; a heat source; shop pencil; old beer bottle; glue trowel and safety goggles.

Materials

- two 4 x 8 sheets of ½-inch treated plywood
- one 4 x 8 sheet of 1½-inch foam insulation
- large sheets of cardboard (to make templates)
- enough 1½-inch PVC pipe (2-inch outside diameter), for four 4- to 5-foot lengths
- PVC pipe straps; rod holder clamps
- Eighteen 1½-inch stainless steel sheet-metal screws to anchor the floor
- ½-inch stainless screws to attach rod holders
- outdoor carpeting and a gallon of carpet glue
- Coleman 40-quart Kwik-Serv cooler
- Super Saver 12-volt aerator
- 10 gauge wire, plugs and ring terminals, and Minn Kota Endura 50 trolling motor, deep-cycle battery and Small Craft Bow Motor Mount

Build Your Own Customized River Boat *continued*

Install the Floor

We wanted the boat to have a floor for several reasons, but primarily because it's easier to walk across a flat floor than the metal boat bottom with exposed ribs. Standing comfort was another factor. Noise abatement is a final and important reason. In any type of fishing, soft "clunks" are better than loud "CLANGS" when you drop a leadhead or open a tacklebox.

Adding the floor is easy. Here's how:

1. Make a cardboard template of the floor. First cut to the overall length and width.

2. Use a compass to measure and mark the cutouts you'll need to make for the ribs. Note that making this cardboard template is not a one-step process. You'll have to try the template several times, making minor adjustments until the fit is perfect.

3. After tracing the template onto your plywood, cut to length and width with a circular saw. Use a jigsaw (right) to make the rib cutouts.

4. Carefully measure the floor space between the ribs of the boat, then mark your foam correspondingly.

5. Cut the foam into pieces that fit between the ribs. The utility knife will cut about halfway through the foam; then simply snap off the measured piece.

6. Place the foam between the ribs. The foam not only adds flotation to the boat, it helps support the plywood floor and deadens accidental noises.

7. Before you place and attach the floor, use it as a template: Lay the floor on the piece of carpet you plan to use, and cut out the general carpet shape: much easier now than when the floor is installed for good. Add 8 inches to the width so 4 inches of carpeting can be glued up each sidewall (Step 9, this page). This prevents small objects from dropping between the flooring and wall. Don't do the final rib cutouts yet.

8. After placing the floor, create a snapline to ensure that you drive screws into the ribs. Drill guide holes (right) to make the task of inserting and tightening screws easier.

9. Fine-tune the carpet fit (make cutouts for ribs after carpet is placed), then roll the carpet back, apply glue to half the floor and re-lay carpet. When smoothing, eliminate all trapped air bubbles before repeating process on the other side. Glue the extra carpet width to the sides of the boat (above), as the finishing touch to laying the carpeting.

Build Your Own Customized River Boat *continued*

Finish Stern Well and Bow Deck

A removable, carpeted floorboard for the stern well provides a quiet place for the fuel tank to ride, yet allows access to the drain plug. We glued the carpet directly to the bow deck; using wood here would simply have added weight to the boat. Here's what to do:

1. Using cardboard, create a template for the stern floorboard.

2. Trace the template shape onto your plywood, then use a circular saw, and jigsaw if needed, to cut out the stern floorboard.

3. Cut a piece of carpet to shape, and leave some excess to wrap over each edge of the board. Glue the carpet to the floorboard, and use a staple gun to secure the wraps to the floorboard's underside.

4. Cut and place foam between ribs of the stern well, then insert your carpeted floorboard.

5. Using cardboard and your utility knife, create a template for the bow deck.

6. From the template, mark and cut carpeting for the bow deck. Leave enough room for wrapping carpeting around back edge of bow deck (arrow).

Deck

Carpet

7. Glue the carpeting directly to the bow deck. Wrap carpeting around back edge of deck, gluing it down (see inset diagram).

Powering Up

Of course, you'll be using your outboard for most of your movements, most notably runs ups and down river. But in actual river fishing, as with other fishing, you'll often want the finesse, precision and quietude that an electric motor offers.

You could install a bow-mount motor, but on the boat we chose that meant building a bracket for the mount. We chose the less complicated route of combining a stern-mount motor with Minn Kota's Small Craft Bow Motor Mount. We like the fact that both the motor and bracket are easy to install and remove.

You'll also see how to power up for a great and simple baitwell.

Here are the details:

1. Clip the terminals from the motor wires and connect a plug, again to facilitate motor removal.

2. Remove the motor head and turn it around so the control handle points into the boat. On the Minn Kota Endura 50, that's a simple matter of removing one bolt, spinning the head and replacing the bolt. This is necessary because you'll be using the motor at the bow and not the stern.

3. Clamp the motor mount to the bow. We found the unit offers a rock-solid spot to mount the motor.

4. Connect a reciprocal plug to two 10-gauge wires, which lead to the floor-mounted battery box just aft of the casting deck. For photographic purposes, we used a battery tray here so you can see how we put the system together, but we recommend you use a box to completely enclose the battery.

5. Attach wires to the floor with wire clips to keep them out of the way.

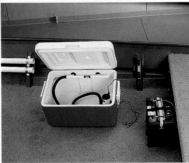

6. Add a bait-well, which is simply a Coleman Kwik-Serv cooler with a hatch in the lid, and a 12-volt Super Saver aerator. The aerator oxygenates the water, and its hose attachment is long enough so you can hang it over the side to pump out stale water and replace with fresh water.

Build Your Own Customized River Boat *continued*

Create Rod Storage

Good rod storage is important in any craft, big or small, to keep your boat uncluttered and protect your rods from damage. While this system won't enclose the entire rod and reel, it certainly protects fragile rodtips, and keeps your expensive sticks out of the way. Here's how to build this simple but effective storage system:

2. To make it easy to insert rodtips into the mounted holders, you'll want to flare one end of the PVC tubes. To start this step, insert 4 inches of the tube into superheated sand.

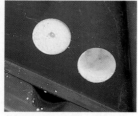

1. Using a 2-inch hole saw, cut holes in the face of the rear seat. If the seat, like ours, is filled with foam flotation (right), twist a section of PVC pipe into the hole to remove a plug about a foot long. It may break off 2 or 3 inches at a time and require several attempts. In a way, the foam is good because it helps stabilize the tubes and keeps them from bouncing around.

3. While the PVC is still hot, press the tube onto an old long-neck beer bottle while it cools. We used a propane cook stove, but you can do it on a kitchen range as well. We found the process frustrating, as sand sometimes became embedded in the PVC, forcing us to remove the affected area and start again. We eventually went to direct heat, holding the end of the pipe just above the flame for about an eight count. This worked well; however, the pipe became discolored in the process and could not be sanded clean. If you use direct heat, do not allow the PVC to burn as the fumes are toxic.

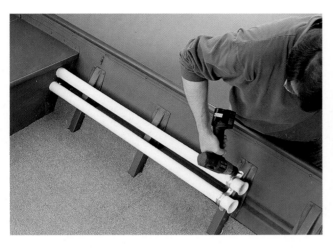

4. After flaring the pipes, cut them to length with a hacksaw. They should be long enough to extend from the rib where they're attached to the boat to at least 10 inches inside the seat. Using the pipe straps, fasten the flared ends to the boat rib.

5. Use a couple of fishing rods to determine where to fasten the butt-holders, then attach them as shown. If you fish spinning gear exclusively, you'll have to stagger the reels when they're in the holder so they don't overlap and bump together. These holders will easily accept 7-foot rods. For the stern fisherman, follow steps 4 and 5 on the other side of the boat, but cut the holes into the face of the bow deck.

Conclusion

There you have it—a boat fit for a river fishing king! It's a little work, but the price of this rig is certainly right, and with these step-by-step instructions you'll know exactly how to bring it all together perfectly and successfully. With a buddy's help, you could probably complete this project in a full day's work, but we prefer the weekend approach: Take your time during some off-season Saturday and Sunday, spin some old fishing tales as you work … and plan some strategy for putting your new rig to work.

What It Costs

Cost was a factor in our project. We not only wanted to keep things simple and light-weight, but also to keep the budget reasonable. Here is what we have into this rig (excluding outboard). Retail prices are taken from a number of sources:

Alumacraft 1542 NCS	$ 1,426
Spartan B-14 Trailer	$ 702
Minn Kota Endura 50 Electric Motor	$ 204
Small Craft Motor Mount	$ 60
Marine Carpet (6x18 feet)	$ 125
Minn Kota MK 20 Deep-cycle Battery	$ 79
Coleman Cooler	$ 27
Super Saver Aerator	$ 33
Rod Holders	$ 20
Humminbird 400 TX Portable Sonar	$ 299
Miscellaneous (Wood/Hardware)	$ 125
Total:	$ 3,100

(plus outboard)

Every fisherman will find tips of value in the pages that follow. Some of these ideas are very specific to a certain species, or a specific type of water. But equally as many of these ideas apply across-the-board, and just represent good thinking on how to be a better and more successful fisherman. Some of these ideas are big, some of them are small ... but all have been proven on the water, by real fisherman, and will help you catch more and bigger fish more often.

Let members and our experts alike be your guides to the little things which add up to big fishing success.

Ho-Ho for Steelheads

For catching steelhead in the tributaries of Lake Erie, nothing works better for me than a rig I concocted.

The bait starts with a size 14 treble hook onto which I put two maggots on each tine of the hook. Then I roll a ¾-inch ball of orange or pink Power Bait and place this onto the black eyelet side of the treble; I squeeze and mold it into a tear-drop shape, pushing down until almost completely covering the tines and most of the maggots.

From the bottom, the hook looks like it is rigged with a Ho-Ho, the snack cake with a cream center. So, I call my rig the Ho-Ho, which has proven to be the most effective bait I have ever used for steelhead fishing.

Thomas J. McGrath III
Pittsburgh, PA

Easy Magazine Library

By saving favorite articles on fishing tips and gear, you can increase your ability to catch fish. Keeping entire magazines creates a clutter. Instead, I use an accordion file-folder that has 31 different compartments. I cut the articles I want to save from the magazines in which they appear. The compartments are separated by species and other categories, such as "Boats and Boat Maintenance," "Fishing Gear," "Clothing," "Lures," "Fishing Tips," "Recipes," "Trolling," etc.

Hank Schlautmann
Port Huron, MI

ADVICE FROM THE PROS

Creatures of Habit

Catfish are creatures of habit. If you start fishing in the morning with cheese, then stay with it. Just because you don't get a bite doesn't mean that they don't like it; they may not be hungry. If you catch catfish in a particular area using a specific bait, don't change. They will bite again on the same bait.

Jimmy Houston
Cookson, OK

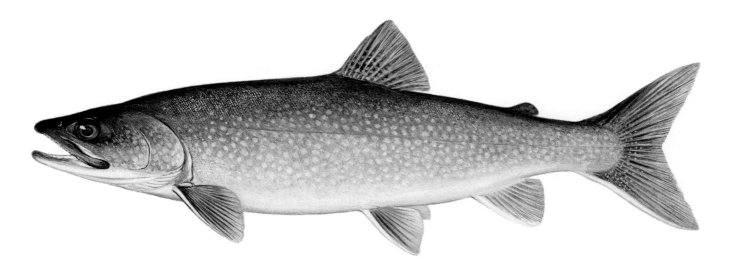

Spring Lake Trout Primer

After ice-out, watch your temperature gauge. Search for water that is warmer by 2 to 5 degrees than most of the body's water. You'll find these hot spots in river mouths, shallows, reefs and areas close to shore. The lakers will be looking for smelt and other baitfish in water that is 44 to 56°F, and they will be hungry.

Now is the time to run your planer boards. Tuck them in close in heavy traffic or rough water. Make them as visible as possible to other boats.

Remember that the vessel coming at you on your port side has the right of way. Don't crowd him, and he may return the courtesy.

Keep an eye out for mud slicks from spring runoff or wave action along shore. This is where your boards will produce. Be alert for floating debris in high water. Watch your speed in these places; save full throttle for later in the season.

Spread out your planer boards and drop your lines well back. After a few passes, give the place a rest. Return later in the day.

Watch for gulls feeding on baitfish that are being driven to the surface. Try to match the size of your lure to the bait size. These lakers soon become boat sensitive.

Don't pass up fish that rise to check the turbulence from your boat and motor. With today's electronics, you can watch these fish come up as much as 20 feet to strike. Experiment setting from 5 to 20 feet deep, 10 to 40 feet back.

The 8-pound cannon balls are good for this shallow fishing—and easier on the equipment too. Keep the weights below the surface to prevent bouncing.

When the fish is in the net, put your thumb on the line, your reel in free spool and your rod in any rod holder, and clear the area. You've just saved half an hour and some broken equipment. If you can turn the net over, dumping the fish on the deck, grab the hook remover, salvage your lure and put the trout back in the lake if you so choose.

Joe Holton
St. George, VT

Helpful Fishing Log

My buddies thought my idea was really silly—until the fall run of huge walleye and white bass came up the Wolf River in Wisconsin. It was a very windy and cold day, and all the guys were talking about how they couldn't remember what lure or presentation they used last year. I pulled out 10 years of what I call my "Weather Fish-Catching Book" and paged through the last 5 years of October fishing and found a day in 1997 that was exactly the same weather conditions as that day. Water temperature was within two degrees and I told them to fish the 12-foot drop with large fathead minnows on a Wolf River rig with a red bead up the line approximately 6 inches. They looked at me and laughed. They came back the next day and were smiling from ear to ear.

"We didn't catch anything doing it our way," they said, "so we decided to try your idea and filled the live well—6 walleyes over 6 pounds and 50 hefty white bass."

Now everybody is keeping a log with the weather, wind speeds, water temperature and moon phases—and what lure or bait they used.

J. T. Tembelis
Appleton, WI

Clean Down to the Bone

To clean fish perfectly, use a teaspoon to scrape the inside of the backbone to which the dark strip of kidney clings. Once the fish is scraped clean, rinse it in cold water and use your fingers to pull away any remaining strands of tissue.

Jacob Sheehan
Eastford, CT

≋ ADVICE FROM THE PROS ≋

Scout Before You Go

The most important stage of your fishing trip may come before you ever throw your first cast. Locate fish by visiting bait shops and boat ramps to talk to guides and local fishermen about where big schools of fish may be found. Buy a topographical map of the body of water and have them mark the spots (✗ marks). Note the type of structure the fish appear to be utilizing and find similar spots on the water. Ask for details about the tactics that are producing.

Ted Takasaki
NAFC Walleye Advisory Council

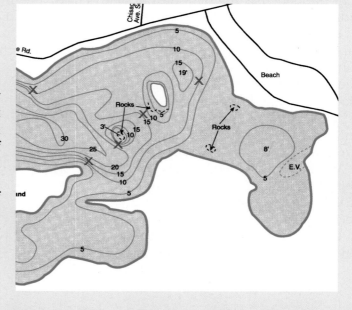

Avoid a Net Loss

I came up with a way to avoid having my net sink if it is dropped into the water. I simply got a can of spray foam insulation and filled the handle. The foam expands, so it is best to drill a hole in the middle of the handle and seal off the ends. A bread knife, incidentally, will cleanly cut off any excess foam after it has dried.

Tim Pleger
Green Bay, WI

Ridding Rust

If you have rust on a metal surface, be it a hook, a boat or whatever, a quick fix is a lead pencil. Keep one handy. Simply mark out rust spots with the pencil, then wipe off the lead and rust with a rag or paper towel.

Rodney Campbell
Murphy, NC

ADVICE FROM THE PROS

Carolina Walleyes

The Carolina rig is a steady walleye catcher, and here is a trick that makes it catch the biggest walleyes around. The usual rigging has a floating lure at the end of the line, and enough clamp-on sinker to take the lure to the bottom, with the lure floating above and behind the sinker.

Here's the walleye wile: Choose a lure that floats with the head pointing downward. When you raise your rod tip sharply, the lure dives toward bottom as if feeding on something. A shopper walleye thinks this critter can be had because it is less wary while feeding. It strikes, and you're suddenly smarter than a giant walleye!

Gene Round
Ocala, FL

Keep Recipes Simple

Both freshwater and saltwater fish have great natural taste. Keep your cooking and ingredients simple. Let's start with a minimum legal snook. Fillet it and skin the fillets. They should divide into about eight serving-size portions. The quickest, easiest and often the best cooking method is to "nuke" it in the microwave. Take a microwave-safe cake pan; separate three of your pieces. Sprinkle with lemon juice, then lightly salt one side of each; put the salted side down, then salt the top lightly. Add a dash of black pepper, paprika, and a couple pats of margarine; then cover and cook on high for 3 minutes. Let rest for 1 minute, then check with fork to see if the thickest part has turned white and flakes easily. If necessary, return to oven at 1 minute intervals until just right. Put the remaining pieces on a baking sheet that has been sprayed with nonstick cooking spray and give them the same seasoning—salt, pepper, paprika, butter and lemon juice. Put in preheated 400°F oven for 6 to 8 minutes.

Col. P. McClain
Pinellas Park, FL

Too Much Lip

When admiring bass, most people grip them by the lower lip and hoist them high in the air. That's okay with average-size fish, but the venerable lip hold may sprain the jaws of bass more than 5 pounds. If a bass fins away with an injured jaw, it may be unable to feed and ultimately die. Once you lip a big bass into the boat, support the fish with your other hand to take the weight off its jaws.

Jacob Sheehan
Eastford, CT

ADVICE FROM THE PROS

Helping Hand for Giant Cats

First, remember that these lurkers got that big by being wary of human scents on baits. The stench of serine, amino acid, on our hands is detected by their eight barbels, or whiskers. These have nearly 200,000 taste buds that can detect scents from as far away as 100 yards upcurrent. So, here's the catching ploy before you begin fishing. Wet your hands and cover them with baking soda. This neutralizes the acid, thus removing any trace of human scent.

Gene Round
Ocala, FL

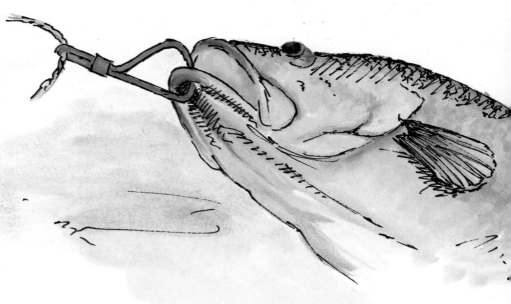

Catch-and-Release Stringer

When I'm catching fish for supper and I use a stringer, I attach the stringer through the fish's bottom lip and not through the gill and mouth. This way, if I want to release the fish, the gills and gill tissue would not be disturbed and it would be easier for the fish to breathe.

Ryan Bertolas
Milwaukee, WI

Cool Aid

Plastic water and soda bottles, emptied of their original contents, then filled with water and frozen, make excellent, cheap reusable ice cubes. There is a bottle size to accommodate almost every need, such as for using with a minnow pail or a huge cooler.

Jeff Grzeskowiak
Marysville, OH

ADVICE FROM THE PROS

Shorter Fights Are Better

Some anglers enjoy a long, drawn-out fight after hooking a fish. Others land it as quickly as possible. They release fish and want them to be as fit as possible to live on.

There are other reasons for quick releases. If you let a fish struggle, it gives off lactic acid, alerting other fish in the school to stop biting. This, also, can adversely affect the flavor of the fish you plan to eat.

Gene Round
Ocala, FL

Fishing Hot Spot

In moving water, the largest fish select locations that offer the best combination of current, oxygen and cover. Look for places where the current channels a concentration of drifting insects, where turbulence aerates the water and where nearby deep water or the shadows of rocks offer secure hiding places. Cast your bait, fly or lure slightly upstream from those big-fish hangouts and let the current take your offering to the fish.

Ben Hankes
Beaver Dam, WI

Ear Protectors Attract Fish

I use foam earplugs used by shooters and factory workers, because they are dense and absorbent, to hold and dispense fish attractant. These earplugs are durable and come in many colors. Simply put a hook through one, place it on or above the hook, squeeze it and spray attractant on it. As the earplug expands back into its shape, it sucks up the attractant.

Sponges don't last as long and they lose scent faster. The earplugs will also raise unweighted baits off the bottom a bit, so fish can see the bait better. Colored earplugs can serve as an additional attractant. I've found that they work in open waters or through the ice.

Edward Mendofik
Ashland, PA

Homemade Marker Buoy

You can use an empty dishwashing liquid bottle as a marker buoy. Spray paint it a bright color, then wrap some heavy string around it and attach a piece of lead to the loose end of the string. It's that simple.

Tim Rehwald
Lawrenceville, IL

ADVICE FROM THE PROS

Summertime Bass

Hot, sultry summer days are a slow time for bass fishing. To bring about a good day's catch, forget the early morning and late afternoon—go at high noon. Find a row of boat docks and just fish the dickens out of each dock. Use small worms, buzzbaits, topwaters and spinnerbaits, but work them thoroughly. Then move out from them to the first cover or breakline, and fish that. These are known habitats for bass in the summer doldrums.

Jimmy Houston
Cookson, OK

Simple Depth Recorder

When you get a bite at a certain depth, take a permanent marker and mark that depth on your line, then drop your line slowly back down to that mark.

Nick J. Moore
Lancaster, TX

Create Fishing Hot Spots

I live in Holiday Shores, a 1,500-acre lake outside Edwardsville, Illinois. Every 5 years, the lake manager lowers the lake so people can repair or build new docks and sea walls. I go around the lake and stack up rocks, riprap, stumps, even Christmas trees to make cover and nesting spots for fish to use. I mark them on a map and fish them!

Darrell Werner
Edwardsville, IL

Life-Saving Throw Device

After watching a fisherman get washed into Lake Michigan by a rogue wave and almost drown, I decided to carry a convenient life-saving device that could be thrown from shore or from a boat. It can be a life saver for pier, bank or ice fishermen, as well as for anglers who fall from boats. The device is easy to make.

In the center of the bottom of a washed-out bleach jug or other heavy-duty jug, with a cone shape, make a hole just large enough to barely pass the end of a 50- to 60-foot length of ¾-inch-diameter nylon rope. Insert the flat rope end through the pour end of the jug and push it through the small hole you made in the bottom. Tie a Bowline Knot or Braid Loop on the end.

Make the loop large enough to go around a person's gloved hand. Push the rest of the flat nylon line into the jug, keeping enough outside the jug to tie or braid a loop at the end.

You have a jug that can be tossed with ease to the victim. The weight of the rope in the jug will allow you to toss it a distance. Be sure to put the loop at the pour end around the wrist of your nonthrowing hand and hold onto it before tossing the device.

Ray Kalisz
Battle Creek, MI

Spice Your Jug

When you are jugging for catfish, fill the jug with cat food and punch holes in the top. You can efficiently chum around your bait.

Eddie Umpfenbach
St. Clair Shores, MI

Make and Mark Crappie Hot Spots

To make a crappie hot spot, first you must attract their main food source—minnows! Cement blocks work well, but are too heavy to transport easily. What works just as well are sections of PVC pipe that are about 2 feet or more in length. Wrap these parallel and sink them at different depths by points and the mouths of creeks, etc. I find them again by shore markers and sonar readings. There will be times when these are the only places where you will catch crappies because they offer a steady source of food.

Steve vonBrandt
Wilmington, DE

≋ ADVICE FROM THE PROS ≋

Mark Structure with Buoys

Whether you are trolling, casting or drifting, the ability to follow structure contours is critical for success. Before wetting a line, use your sonar to follow drop-offs and weedlines. Place plastic marker buoys, commercially sold or homemade, that feature an anchor rope and reasonably weighted anchor, to highlight subtle turns and points that hold fish. They give you a target to which to cast or guide your trolling path.

Ted Takasaki
NAFC Walleye Advisory Council

Balloons As Floats

Tired of losing expensive floats while fishing in heavy cover or not having the right size float when you need it? No problem; the solution is simple and easy.

Just find an ordinary latex balloon and fill it with air. If you get hung up, you can always buy another dozen for the price of a single balsa-wood float. If the fish are finicky, you can downsize the balloon just by letting the air out. If the fish happen to be just out of reach, set up downwind and let the wind carry your balloon and bait right up to the fish's mouth.

Do you like night fishing? Place a replacement glow tube from some of those expensive light-up bobbers in the balloon before inflating, and you have a night bobber that will last well into the next day. I have used this method for a couple of years now and have landed various species including smallmouth and largemouth bass, catfish, panfish and walleye. All you need to do is attach the balloon by tying it directly to the line. Those of us who use larger baits, such as bluegill and suckers, will appreciate the fact that the bait cannot pull the float under and it keeps the bait in the productive zone. To aid in casting, extra weight may be applied. If you are getting strikes, but the fish seem to be letting go too soon, let some air out so the fish do not feel as much resistance. Try changing balloon color at night to see if the different colors give you different reactions.

Ed Lorentz
Pittsburgh, PA

ADVICE FROM THE PROS

Estimating Bass Weights

Here's a surprisingly accurate method to estimate the weight of most largemouth bass. Measure the length, deduct 10, then divide by 2. For example, a 14-inch bass should weigh 2 pounds, and it will, within an ounce or so. A 20-incher approximates 5 pounds. Bass over 20 inches won't conform because of a variance in pot bellies.

No ruler handy? Use a dollar bill; it is 6⅛ inches long.

Gene Round
Ocala, FL

Poor Man's Depth Probe

To determine the water clarity and its temperature at fishing depth, I have put together a poor man's depth probe. I took a swimming pool thermometer, which costs less than $10, and painted the top chartreuse. I then took some strong cord and tied it to the top of the thermometer, along with a 2-ounce sinker, which I also painted chartreuse. Next, I tied a knot at 2-foot intervals along the rest of the cord.

To determine water clarity, I lower the thermometer until I can't see the top and the sinker. I then count the number of feet of cord I have out. Zero to 1 feet means muddy water. One to 3 feet is stained. If I can see the top beyond 3 feet, the water is clear.

The thermometer tells me water temperature down to 8 feet, which gives me an idea of how active the bass should be.

My poor man's depth probe is cheap, simple and, best of all, it works.

Michael J. Dumiak
Santer, SC

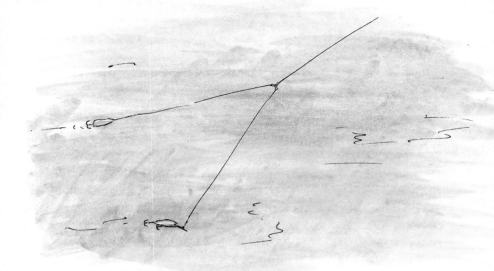

When Singles Are Better Than Triples

When I go trout fishing, I always carry a couple of spoons with the treble hook removed and replaced with a single hook. When I'm not catching fish with a regular spoon, I will put a live minnow on the single-hook spoon. That will often trigger a strike, and the single hooks are more gentle on the trout.

Josh Estep
Elizabethton, TN

Double Your Chances

While trolling for gamefish, you can double your chances for attracting more strikes. Take a three-way swivel and tie a 20- to 30-inch leader to one swivel. To that add your favorite diving crankbait. To the second swivel, add a 36-inch leader and tie on one of your favorite spoons. The third swivel, of course, goes to the snap on the end of your main line. The crankbait will dive to its own level, and the spoon will trail just above. This creates two situations. First, it gives you two baits in the water on one rod and, second, it imitates one baitfish pursuing another, something other fish usually cannot resist. The only real "trick" to this is that you must allow the crankbait to "dig in" first, then pitch the spoon in gently behind the crankbait, taking care not to foul the spoon line around itself—much easier than it sounds, and successful, too. I have found myself fighting doubles many times.

Herman Kunz
Fairfield, IL

≋ ADVICE FROM THE PROS ≋

Follow the Wind

Windy days are sometimes a nuisance to fishermen, but they really are a friend. In the hot summer months, a windy bank will be loaded with forage, and the bass will move in to feed on that forage. But don't run to that bank as soon as the wind blows. Give the wind time to blow the forage into that bank. Then go there in about an hour or so.

Jimmy Houston
Cookson, OK

Give Them Away

During the really hot weather, go through your tackle box and sort out all the lures and tackle you never use and give them to the first kid you see fishing. The reward you get from the child's smile will be worth more than all your old lures!

Steve vonBrandt
Wilmington, DE

Bass on the Edge

All predators, including bass, gravitate to natural edges—places where one type of habitat intersects with another. Good examples of edges in your home lake include the area where a weedline meets open water, a shoreline where mud changes to gravel and a drop-off from 5 to 20 feet. Bass station themselves close to such edges because forage opportunities tend to be greater there.

Don Wirth
Nashville, TN

Backup Help

Many times while throwing spinnerbaits, buzzbaits or ripping jerkbaits, bass will take a swipe at your lure without touching a hook. The fish may try again, so keep a backup rod rigged with tubebaits, worms or soft jerkbaits that have plenty of scent or attractant on hand. Get your first line in quickly and throw the plastic back to the spot the bass attacked your lure. The fish will take the plastic more often than the original lure that drew the strike.

William McCabe
Napa, CA

Lemon Deodorizer

I have found an easy way to get that "fish smell" off of your hands. When washing them, apply a liberal amount of lemon juice to your hands. Repeat a few times, if necessary. The fish smell will quickly disappear.

Brandon K. Hutchinson
Mt. Vernon, IN

Stocking Stuffer

Here is a tip for a Christmas stocking stuffer. I've put some worm hooks, leadheads and plastic worms in the boys' stockings every year since they were old enough to fish. Last year I wanted to add something a little different and special.

I bought some 3-inch stainless-steel nail clippers and I engraved their initials and the year on the back. I found their favorite college team logo lanyards and put them together.

The kids wear the clippers around their neck for trimming ends and to show school spirit while fishing. With their names on the back, there is no confusion as to whose clipper it is.

Rick Evans
Odessa, FL

The Long-Distance Cast

A lot of tricks can add some distance to your cast, but none will make a dramatic difference. To get your lure or bait way out there, you need specialized equipment. I put together a combination that will put your offering well beyond average distance.

I use an 8-foot 6-inch medium-light downrigger rod with a light spinning reel capacity of 130 yards of 8-pound test. Load 40 yards of 8-pound-test mono for a base, then fill the spool with super braid line. (Cabela's Ripcord SI works great: 15-pound test has a silicone coating and the same diameter as 2-pound mono.) Attach another 15 to 20 feet of 8- to 10-pound-test fluorocarbon to the braid by using a closely trimmed nail knot. Add the leader you desire.

Downrigger rods have a very slow action, making a dramatic bend as you start the cast. The rod will whip forward and catapult your bait a great distance. Line drag is minimized with the small-diameter braid, and low stretch is necessary with that much line out. The 8- to 10-pound-test fluorocarbon at the end has the strength to withstand the initial strain of the cast. For bottom fishing, try a ½- to 1-ounce sliding-sinker rig. When casting for surface-feeding fish, use a clear plastic torpedo bobber with a 3-foot leader and a small jog, streamer fly or plastic minnow. The distance you will cast is amazing.

William McCabe
Napa, CA

Charter Fish Fighting Tips

When a fish strikes, you have to be quick and prepared. Know ahead of time who is first, second and third. Reel while the rod remains in the rod holder until you catch up to the fish. Then take the rod smoothly out of the rod holder—do not yank—and get your rod tip up and keep it there.

Do not look at the reel. Just keep pressure on the fish and keep the rod tip bent to the same degree, no matter whether the fish is going away, coming at you or doing any number of tricks.

Do not tighten the drag. It should be set so that you have a shot at a fish simply hooked in the lip. Don't worry if the fish is taking line. That's what the game is all about. You can pull the other lines and chase him. You can help by pointing the rod at the fish, tip high. Stay in the back of the boat.

Keep your line out of the prop and away from the down-rigger cables.

Joe Holton
St. George, VT

Packing Checklist

Make a fishing trip packing checklist for your convenience. Include sections on fishing tackle, safety gear, personal items, snacks and boating needs. Save it on your computer and keep copies handy with your tackle.

Dennis Malkin
Gates Mills, OH

≋ ADVICE FROM THE PROS ≋

River Hangouts for Walleyes

Find walleyes in rivers by searching for anything that diverts current and creates slow-water areas called eddies, where game-fish rest and lie in wait for food. Eddies form in places like the upstream side of wingdams, on either side of points that jut out from the shoreline, in bridge abutments, behind fallen or flooded trees and where feeder creeks empty into the main stream. Depressions in the bottom also hold fish. Springtime walleyes stage in hard-bottom spots on the inside turns of river bends, where water moves more slowly. In fall, check turns with irregular bottoms.

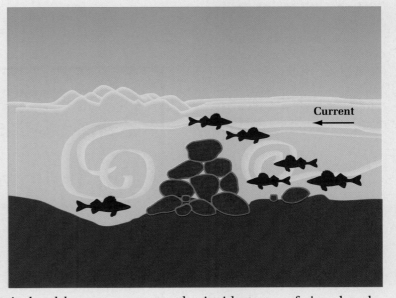

Current

Ted Takasaki
NAFC Walleye Advisory Council

Before You Cook Your Fish

After catching and cleaning fish, I fillet them or, if they are too small, I'll scale and gut them. What I do next really improves the flavor of the fish I cook.

Put the fish in a glass bowl. Sprinkle salt on fillets or, for fish not filleted, in cavities and surfaces. Cover with water and soak for 24 hours in the refrigerator. Then take the fish out and rinse it thoroughly with cold water.

Cook the fish as desired or freeze it in a freezer bag filled with water. The salt solution cleans out any missed blood, oil, etc., to help ensure great-tasting fish.

Randy Jacobs
Lubbock, TX

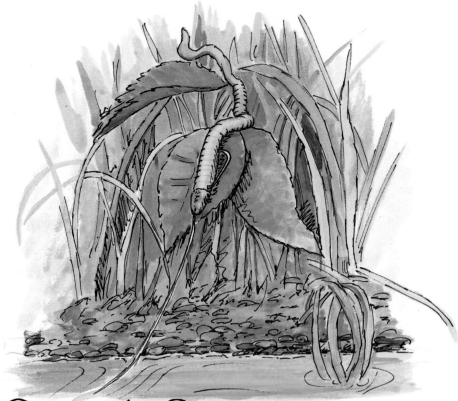

Cast on the Grass

To catch the attention of bass holding close to the shore, pitch your weedless lures into the grass growing along the bank and shake the vegetation before pulling your lure into the water.

Jacob Sheehan
Eastford, CT

ADVICE FROM THE PROS

Put Followers on Your Leader

When you see a fish follow your lure, then turn away, it's because that fish is wary about something. Cast to the same spot, and halfway back, suddenly cease reeling and let the lure settle to bottom. Make a slow ten count, then jerk the lure off bottom and retrieve as fast as you can. This can trigger impulse strikes.

Gene Round
Ocala, FL

Trophy Chain Pickerel

Have you been trying to catch trophy chain pickerel, but they somehow always elude you? When I say "trophy," I am talking about fish that are over 4½ pounds. A 4-pound chain pickerel is really a nice fish for the Northeast. The record for most New England states is less than 8 pounds.

The first thing you will need in the way of equipment is lots of cold-weather clothes! That's right, cold-weather clothes. You will be fishing for these fish in December, January and February!

First, survey the lakes you will be fishing now to locate grassbeds with deep water nearby.

Second, you will need a variety of jigs from ⅟64 to ⅛ ounce. You will need some marabou jigs in brown and black, some shad darts, and some leadhead jig heads, painted in black and white, and some plastic-body grubs, in the 1½- to 2-inch size, in white, yellow and green.

Rig up two or three rods with a different size and color grub on each one. Then, locate the weedbeds you found earlier in the year, and position the boat so that you can drift over these areas sideways with the wind. You should drift slowly enough to keep your jigs near the bottom, and sometimes bouncing bottom. If you drift too fast, slow the boat with your electric motor or a drift sock. Drift two poles out the side of the boat while you cast with the other. Be careful watching your line as you drift. When the line does anything that it hasn't been doing, pick up the pole and slowly apply pressure to the line, with a slight snap of your wrist. Be careful not to set the hook too hard or you will lose it and break your line.

If you still can't locate any pickerel after several hours of this method in your best areas, then put out only one pole in the back of the boat, with a brown, ⅛-ounce hairy jig, and troll in wide 360° circles over the area. Watch your line. When they take the jig, it will appear as if the jig is caught on grass, but it isn't. Pick up the pole, but don't set the hook. Just apply steady pressure and hang on for the fight of your life.

One day in January 1993, while fishing a local lake using these methods, my son and I caught eight chain pickerel over 4 pounds in just 5 hours, with a 34°F air temperature and a 25 to 30 mph wind. The largest fish was a little over 5 pounds, and took the "Best in Species" award for *Sports Afield* for the year.

So, this winter, when everyone has cabin fever, pick up your rod and tackle box and head for your favorite lake. You just might catch the next state record pickerel.

Steve vonBrandt
Wilmington, DE

Back-Handed Application

When applying insect repellent, make sure to use the backs of your hands, so as not to get any on your lures. It can give your lures an offensive smell and can ruin the finish.

Aaron Turner
Presque Isle, MI

Weather Clues

During a cold front, watch the clouds and follow these guidelines:

Stalled and Overcast: Look for bass in the shallows

Clear Sky: Bass move deep

Fluffy Clouds (cumulus): Front has passed; bass resume normal feeding

Thunderheads: Bass are at feeding peaks

High, Thin Clouds (cirrus): Bass feed heavily

Andy Schneider
Carmel, IN

Bank Fishing for Cats at Night

I do a lot of bank fishing at night for catfish, and I've acquired a lot of experience. Maybe these tips will help you.

• Fish with the line slack and set the drag loose.

• Paint rod tiptops with white enamel model paint. White is a nice contrast against dark waters at night.

• In spring and early summer, raw shrimp is an excellent cut bait. We use them, fresh or frozen, with the shell still attached. We use a 4/0 Eagle Claw bait-holder hook, 17-pound-test Stren Low Visibility and a 30-pound-test, 18- to 30-inch Spider Line leader. Shrimp can be fished on a bobber, if you prefer.

• The best way to fish raw shrimp is when it's spoiled; we let it "cure" in the garage for a couple of days or until it turns a light pink color.

• Always take more than one bait. What cats fed on the previous night might not be the bait they want tonight.

Anthony Hyde
Cerro Gordo, IL

≋ ADVICE FROM THE PROS ≋

Gentle Release

When releasing bass, don't pitch them. Just gently release them into the water, touching as little of their body as possible. If it is a big bass, 5 pounds or better, move the bass around and let it breathe a little. Then scoot it into the water. If it floats back up, put it in your live well, and turn on the aerator; the added oxygen will help rejuvenate it. You don't have to kiss them like I do on my television show, but be gentle and release them with ease.

Jimmy Houston
Cookson, OK

Create a Walleye Hot Spot

Walleye fishermen should set up a bright light and point it at the water. After a few nights, the baitfish will be attracted to the light. The walleye will follow the baitfish, and you will have yourself a prime spot to catch some late-night walleye. Check local regulations to make sure this is legal where you fish.

Kory Klatt
River Falls, WI

Think Small

Too many times, small waters are overlooked by anglers. Runoff ponds, flooded backwaters, creeks and streams are easily accessed and often hold a lot of fish. They may not be record breakers, but with a box full of jigs, small crankbaits and spinners, you can really have some fun with smallmouth bass, bluegills, trout and even creek chubs. Such waters are especially good for getting kids started, when you want to make sure they catch some fish.

Mark Johnson
Tiskilwa, IL

ADVICE FROM THE PROS

Go Northwest, Young Man

In early spring, the northwest corner of the lake is your best bet for a lunker bass. The water here will typically be 5 degrees warmer than elsewhere in the lake, because cold north winds tend to blow over this area and hit with greater severity on the opposite shore. The earliest weed growth will also appear in the northwest corner, further increasing its appeal to bass.

Don Wirth
Nashville, TN

Early Steelhead Warning System

When fishing for steelhead in the tributaries of Lake Erie, most night fishermen fish off the bottom and usually hook a bobber in the open, or sliding, position on the line between the tip and the last eyelet as a strike indicator. Some use little bells hooked to the rod tip or lightsticks attached to the rod tip.

These methods work well to indicate a strike. During the fight, however, the bobber or bell usually adds drag to the line or, worse, gets caught up in the line. The result: You just lost the fish of a lifetime.

A very simple and inexpensive solution to this problem has doubled the number of night-time steelies I've landed. Here's what to do:

Go to a toy store and purchase a three-pack of brightly colored PlayDoh. I keep a can of fluorescent green, red and orange in my tackle bag. After casting to that perfect spot and letting the split-shot settle on the bottom, pull in the slack and set the rod in the rod holder. Once you are set up, grasp the line between the rod tip and the next guide, and pull that line down about 12 inches. Then pinch off ¾ inch of PlayDoh and roll it into a ball. Squeeze that ball onto the line, letting it hang down below the rod. Now you have a very bright strike indicator, and when you set the hook and start fighting the monster fish, the PlayDoh falls safely away and will not interfere with your drag or get tangled in your line.

Thomas J. McGrath III
Pittsburgh, PA

Rule of Thumb

Filleting crappie, perch and sunfish may be the best way to prepare them, but when it comes to scaling the fish, I am all thumbs.

Here's what I mean. After cleaning and gutting a day's catch of panfish, I put them in a bucket of cold water. While holding a fish in the bucket, I run my thumb from the tail toward the head, applying light pressure as I do. The scales come right off and sink to the bottom of the bucket. In no time, I have all of the fish scaled and ready for the frying pan.

Sean Carpenter
Milwaukee, WI

≈ ADVICE FROM ≈ THE PROS

Cleaning Up in Dirty Water

Runoff can muddy rivers, lakes and reservoirs after a period of hard rain. Water clarity becomes key. Areas near dams tend to clear faster because dirt particles have more time to settle before reaching them. In rivers, look for feeder creeks draining harder-bottom areas or water discharges from factories and powerplants. You can often see a distinct mud line extending into the main waterway. Try fishing it. Last, bulk up your baits and try rattles to add sound to your presentation.

Ted Takasaki
NAFC Walleye Advisory Council

Getting the Big White Bass

White bass travel in schools, and the sizes run from a few to several pounds. Here's how to catch the whoppers:

When you see a school feeding on the surface, watch patiently and see what direction it is traveling. Move ahead of the roving school and sit quietly, staying a long cast away. As the school gets within casting distance, fire a heavy jig or spoon past the head of the school and let it sink for a ten count. It will sink below the main school, where the older, wiser, bigger lunkers hang out for an easy meal. They pick up the dying, sinking shad that the school wounds in its slashing attacks.

Gene Round
Ocala, FL

Tailwater Stripers

Tailwater stripers feed most heavily right after water releases from the dam. Call ahead to the powerhouse and be there, ready to cast your lure, as soon as the releases begin!

Steve vonBrandt
Wilmington, DE

Jig Bag

Any jigs that I use on an outing are kept in a small plastic bag until I get home. I rinse them and dry them before I put them back with my other, unused jigs. This keeps moisture out of my plastic boxes and prevents rusting of my jigs. This is especially helpful when I have fished in saltwater, but it is a useful plan in freshwater as well. After the jigs are dry, I inspect them to see which ones might need repainting, and I also check for hooks that need sharpening. This way, anything in my plastic box is ready to be used, with no lost fishing time from sharpening.

Russ Gough
Key West, FL

No Bones About It

If you are like me, you love to eat fish, but you hate to fight with bones. Here's what you need to do:

When you are ready to fry your fish, take a slab and score it almost all the way through. Do this every half inch. I use corn meal and flour as a batter after I dip the fish in egg. I then deep fry the fish in olive oil until they are golden brown or when they float to the top of the pan.

By scoring them, then deep frying the fish, the hot oil softens the bones. They will crumble and can be eaten without getting caught in your throat.

Paul L. Winstead Jr.
Mt. Vernon, OH

Avoid a Fray

When using nylon string on your trot lines, melt the edges of nylon between the clips/swivels and the hooks to keep it from fraying.

Henry Julo
Atchison, KS

≋ ADVICE FROM THE PROS ≋

Photo Tips with a Flash

When photographing in the bright sunlight, harsh shadows come into the photos quite easily. Set your camera to manual, and manually use the flash. The added light will fill the dark crevices and give a more realistic photo, without the harsh shadows. If you have automatic metering, the camera will meter the subject for the bright light. After you see the setting, stop your camera down one more stop and reap the rewards of a great shot.

Jimmy Houston
Cookson, OK

With flash

Without flash

Muddy-Water Bass

Don't let high, muddy water spoil your next bassin' trip to your favorite river. Position your boat close to a rocky or stumpy bank and cast a jig 'n' pig or large crankbait right against the shoreline. Often a bass will nail the lure on the first turn of the reel handle. Under these conditions, bass will stick very close to current breaks such as rocks, riprap and laydown logs, and will have an extremely small strike zone. Use a bulky lure for maximum visibility, and make sure your bait contacts the cover.

Don Wirth
Nashville, TN

Catch a Break

A great place to catch a lot of fish may be closer than you think. A marina with breakwalls on the Great Lakes can offer excellent fishing for anything. I've caught bass, pike, messes of very large panfish, salmon, walleye, trout and even muskie fishing off of the breakwalls near my house.

Aaron Turner
Presque Isle, MI

Line Your Gloves

Layering clothing in cold weather is the best way to stay warm. Though everyone knows this, I rarely see people apply this knowledge to the first part of your body to get cold—your hands. Put glove liners on before your mittens or gloves, and you'll be twice as warm.

Jeff Grzeskowiak
Marysville, OH

High and Dry

If your fish cooler has no drain, place a raised grid in the bottom of the cooler. Pour crushed ice on the grid. When you place fish in the cooler, the ice will melt, the fish will stay cold, and the fish will not soak up any of the water from the melted ice, which could reduce the flavor.

Patrick Richter
Dayton, OH

Cheap, Easy Fish Stringer

Before you throw out that old electrical radio, appliance or tool, save the cord. Cut the prongs from the plug and tie a common overhand knot about 8 inches from the plug end. Feed the plug through the knot and cinch down. This makes a loop, because the plug won't pass through the knot. Feed the other end through the fish's gills, then back through the loop. The cord makes an excellent fish stringer.

William McCabe
Napa, CA

Be Different

Sometimes all you have to do to catch more and bigger bass is to NOT DO what everyone else is doing. Bass really do become conditioned to seeing certain lures at certain speeds, in certain areas. Try using something completely different from what everyone else is using, such as a big topwater bait with props. You will really be surprised at what you catch.

Steve vonBrandt
Wilmington, DE

≋ ADVICE FROM THE PROS ≋

Clear Look at Visibility Factor

Having some idea of how far a fish can see can help you catch more, especially bass, pike, walleye, white bass and muskies. Here is a simple way to make your own light meter:

The average visibility across America is a few feet. To check what it is where you fish, rig a white or yellow lure, reel it against the rod tip and shove it downward. If it disappears a few inches under the surface, visibility is poor. Use lures that appeal to a fish's sonar sense, like rattlers or vibrators.

If the bright lure disappears 2 or 3 feet down, visibility is normal; try all color patterns to see which ones the fish want.

If the bright lure is visible at 5 to 6 feet, visibility is maximum; use natural patterns, like shiner, shad, bluegill and perch. Retrieve lures very slowly in murky water, faster in clear.

Gene Round
Ocala, FL

Foil Crankbait Snags

My crankbaits would often snag on the boat deck, other rods, line and lures, so to solve that problem, I now take some aluminum foil along with me and wrap it around the lure—hooks and all. When I am traveling and want to keep my lures on the line, I take a sheet of aluminum foil about 12 inches long, fold it in half, and wrap it around the rod, line and lure all at once. It's easy to unwrap, reuse, and if it is unusable, you can always take several sheets and store them in the top of your tackle box, conforming to the inside lid, and they are readily available, at any time.

Stanley R. Chandler
Niceville, FL

ADVICE FROM THE PROS

Pickerel May Knock Twice

Eastern chain pickerel may be one of the smallest members of the pike family, but they are as voracious as any of their big cousins. If you cast and hook a pickerel, then lose him, don't hesitate to cast right back to the spot where he hit.

Pickerel will often return to their original lair, and they frequently follow up a hit on one cast with another on the next.

Glenn Sapir
Putnam Valley, NY

This Sounds Corny

If you know a place where trout have been stocked, take a few handful of corn kernels and toss them into the water. Then set your bobber about a foot from the bottom. Use two waxworms for bait on a small hook.

Get ready for action!

Bill Stalego
Newark, OH

Clear-Water Bobber

In clear water, where fish may be especially spooky, I've been rigging for the conditions. I use fluorocarbon line or leader, which works fine. The problem was the bobber or float system.

I guess I could have used the clear-plastic bubbles manufactured for fishing flies with spinning tackle, but I found an easy-to-use and cheap-to-obtain alternative. I use different-size bubble wrap. I cut out individual bubbles, or for trolling, a strip of small bubbles. Simply thread on the bubbles carefully so that you don't pop them. It is nearly invisible.

Steve Reeck
Fargo, ND

Fat-Reduced Grilled Trout or Salmon

Here's a tip on how to cook a trout or salmon once you've caught and filleted it:

INGREDIENTS:

1 large trout or salmon fillet, skinned
1 small to medium onion, sliced
Yellow or brown mustard
Ketchup or barbecue sauce
1-2 T. lemon juice
1-2 T. Lowry's seasoning salt
Salt and pepper to taste
3-4 pats of butter or margarine

Preheat your grill on a medium-heat setting. Remove the dark meat or strip from the skinned side of the fillet. Place your fillet, skinned side down, on aluminum foil. Gently make slices about 1 to 2 inches apart three-quarters of the way through the fish, the entire length of the fillet. Sprinkle with lemon juice and seasoning salt. Place the onion slices the length of the fillet and squirt a moderate amount of mustard and ketchup over the top. (Barbecue sauce is optional.) Salt and pepper lightly and place the pats of butter evenly spaced along the top. Place another piece of foil over the top and seal the edges to make a completely closed package. Carefully flip the fillet over and make several small fork pokes to accommodate fat drainage. Flip it back over and repeat the fork poke routine to make steam vents. Place this package on your grill rack at medium temperature for about 15 minutes. Carefully open the top, exposing the whole fillet, and cook another 10-15 minutes until tender and juicy. Cooking times will vary depending on the thickness of the fillet. Serve this with fat-free ranch dressing, instead of tartar sauce, for a heart-smart dinner.

Rex Ballard
Benzonia, MI

Odor-Free Fish-Cleaning Aftermath

After cleaning fish, to keep the guts from stinking up the place until the next trash pickup day, simply seal them in a zip-top plastic bag and put the bag in the freezer. Don't forget to add the frozen guts to the garbage just before the next collection.

Patrick Richter
Dayton, OH

Tip for Better Tasting Salmon

Central California salmon season opens in late winter/early spring, before the large schools of baitfish begin to show. The salmon must feed on tightly packed schools of a zooplankton called krill. Acids from the krill have a detrimental effect on the flavor and texture of salmon, so when you land an early-season salmon, clean the fish as soon as possible. Pack the fish in ice to preserve maximum freshness and flavor.

William L. McCabe
Napa, CA

Lure Retriever Rig

I recently purchased a lure retriever for under $10 and bought 30 feet of small-diameter poly rope very inexpensively to go with the retriever. I kept having trouble keeping the loose rope stored neatly, however. So I purchased the cheapest fly reel I could find, which cost less than $10. It kept everything wound up until I needed it.

The whole rig cost less than $20 and paid for itself the first day I used it.

J. Kevin Edwards
Danville, AL

≈ ADVICE FROM THE PROS ≈

Willow Trees for Bluegills

When fishing for bluegills, find a willow tree along the bank and fish under it. The insects that feed on the plentiful sap of a willow drop to the water below and are a fish's gourmet delight. In the late spring during the mayfly hatch, these trees hide a bounty of bluegills.

Jimmy Houston
Cookson, OK

Dig Out the Cane Pole

The next time your favorite panfish lake becomes weed choked and difficult to fish, dig out your 12-plus-foot-long cane pole. Tie on about 6 feet of six-pound-test line, a No. 10 hook and a small split shot; leave off the bobber. The bait is your choice.

Using a canoe or a small boat with a quiet electric motor, sneak along the weed edge and probe the tiny holes that exist in all weeds. A hole the size of your hand often holds a fish the same size.

Remember: quiet is key.

Rex Ballard
Benzonia, MI

Lighted Fishing Marker

A great way to mark or locate your favorite fishing locations at night is to place a 4-inch-long cyalume lightstick in a plastic 20-ounce clear beverage bottle. Tie on a 30-foot piece of heavy monofilament, from 14- to 20-pound-test, and add a 2-ounce sinker to serve as an anchor to hold your marker in place.

Matt Radzialowski
Wixom, MI

Lite Trout Recipe

For health reasons, I am restricted to a low-fat, low-cholesterol, low-salt diet. Other members may be in the same situation, and I am sure they will appreciate this recipe for trout.

1. Skin the trout. It is easier to skin it if you put it in the freezer for about 20 minutes. This stiffens the fish and makes it easier to handle.

2. Cut away the belly fat. On most trout, everything from the bottom of the ribs to the belly is full of fat.

3. With the edge of your knife scrape away the roll of fat along the outside of the backbone of the fish.

4. Thoroughly rinse the fish inside and out, then lightly season the meat with black pepper. I then apply a liberal coating of "Mrs. Dash" salt substitute.

5. Line a shallow pan with aluminum foil and place a cake cooling rack in the pan.

6. Place the fish on the rack and tightly cover with aluminum foil. This keeps the fish from drying out.

7. Bake at 350°F until done. (Done is when the flesh easily separates from the backbone when lifted with a fork.) Two 12-inch trout take 40-45 minutes; a six-pound trout will take 75-90 minutes.

Cooking the trout this way on a rack allows the fat and oils to drip off the meat. The resulting trout tastes lighter, less fishy and less oily, plus you haven't added any fats as you would if you fried it. If someone in your family doesn't ordinarily like fish, this preparation may surprise them.

Matt Jacobson
Post Falls, ID

Tasty Crappies

Everyone has his own favorite recipe for crappies, which always are great on the table. Here's my fast and easy preparation:

INGREDIENTS:

> 1 box of noodle helper Alfredo
> Filleted crappies cut into one-inch chunks
> Olive oil
> Garlic powder
> Oregano

Coat a nonstick frying pan with olive oil. Heat oil and add the fish. Sprinkle on garlic powder and oregano. Fry, turning every few minutes, until flaky. Make noodles as instructed on box. When you come to step calling for covering the noodles, add fish, cover and simmer.

This must taste all right, because my kids even like it. I always accompany this with corn as the vegetable and homemade or Italian-style bread.

Howard Reges
Butler, PA

For a Cleaner Cooler

To keep a foam-plastic fish cooler from "sweating through" as the ice inside melts, line it with a plastic garbage bag before filling it. The bag also helps keep the cooler clean.

Patrick Richter
Dayton, OH

≈ ADVICE FROM THE PROS ≈

Buzzbait Buzz

When fishing with a buzzbait, don't use a rod that's overly stiff; you may react too quickly when a bass strikes and pull the lure out of its mouth. Use a rod with a fairly light tip; this gives the bass a split second to inhale the lure before you can react with a hookset. Also, keep handy a spare rod rigged with a floating plastic worm; if a bass boils on the buzzbait and misses it, immediately cast the floating worm to the spot, and it'll usually get eaten.

Don Wirth
Nashville, TN

TACTICS & HINTS

Keep a Fishing Log

Keep a complete and thorough fishing log of all your trips, good and bad. Note location, time of day, water and surface temperature, water clarity and depth, weather, baits used, what worked and what didn't. They are very useful for looking back and seeing what worked for that particular water or condition, and it allows you to relive great fishing memories.

J. Kevin Edwards
Danville, AL

Power Line for Cats

When I was a kid we used to use a special rig we called a "power line." It was dynamite on catfish.

It consisted of a 3- or 4-pound weight, a 12-foot-long heavy-duty rubber band/bungee cord, a leader and 10 to 15 feet of heavy cord. It was the best catfish catcher I've ever seen, because you could feel the fish brushing up against the rig just before it struck.

We'd tie the rubberband to the weight and leader. We'd tie the cord to the other end of the leader. We'd hold the cord about 3 feet from its end, wrapping it around one hand once or twice.

Then we'd throw the weight out far enough to pull the whole line taut. Next, we'd pull the cord in to put our baited hooks on the leaders. I always used nightcrawlers cut in thirds on size 8 Eagle Claw hooks. Then we'd let the rubberband take the three rigs back out. From then on, it was a matter of holding the cord and feeling for the fish to arrive.

My uncle used to use Limburger cheese and fox tail rolled into balls the size of a .44 slug. Nightcrawlers and his concoction were both lethal. We never came home with less than our limits.

Chris Autrey
Grand Terrace, CA

≋ ADVICE FROM THE PROS ≋

Prespawn Largemouths

Spawning is a crucial time for largemouth bass. Fishing for them prior to the spawn is the best time for a catch of a lifetime. As these bass stage they move about quite openly and randomly, but they can usually be found in 4 to 7 feet of water. So, when beginning your spring fishing, start and stay in that depth. You will be duly rewarded with nice catches—but release them! They are the future of fishing.

Jimmy Houston
Cookson, OK

Double Up on White Bass

A good way to get a double hookup on white bass is to have one angler keep a lure ready after the other person hooks a fish. As the white struggles against the hook, cast near it, and a strike from a fish following it should result.

Steve vonBrandt
Wilmington, DE

Weigh and Release

To safely and easily weigh your trophy fish before release, leave it in the net and hook the scale onto the net. This is especially beneficial to delicate-mouthed fish like trout. But no cheating: remember to subtract the weight of the net from the total.

Alan Vormelker
Cleveland, OH

Airplane Fish Finder?

To increase your chance of catching fish, check for jet trails in the sky. I have found that if there are jet trails, go fishing; no jet trails, go swimming, play golf or do something else. It must have something to do with atmospheric pressure. All I know is that this rule of thumb has proven to be a reliable fishing barometer.

Casey Spranger
Ft. Wayne, IN

≋ ADVICE FROM THE PROS ≋

Bass Bonanza in Muddy Water

A sudden influx of muddy water can result in a bass bonanza in a normally clear reservoir. The muddy runoff will carry worms and insects with it, setting up a major bass feeding scenario. After a heavy rain, head for the back of an inflowing tributary and fish the muddy water there with a hard-vibrating lure, such as a Rat-L-Trap or a spinnerbait with Colorado blades.

Don Wirth
Nashville, TN

Index